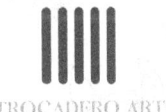
TROCADERO ART

Copyright © 2020 By H. Elmir

All rights reserved. This book or parts thereof may not be reproduced in any form, stored in any retrieval system, or transmitted in any form by any means electronic, mechanical, photocopy, recording, or otherwise without prior written permission of the publisher, except as provided by United States of America copyright law.

ISBN: 9798588002431

Printed by AMAZON.
www.amazon.com

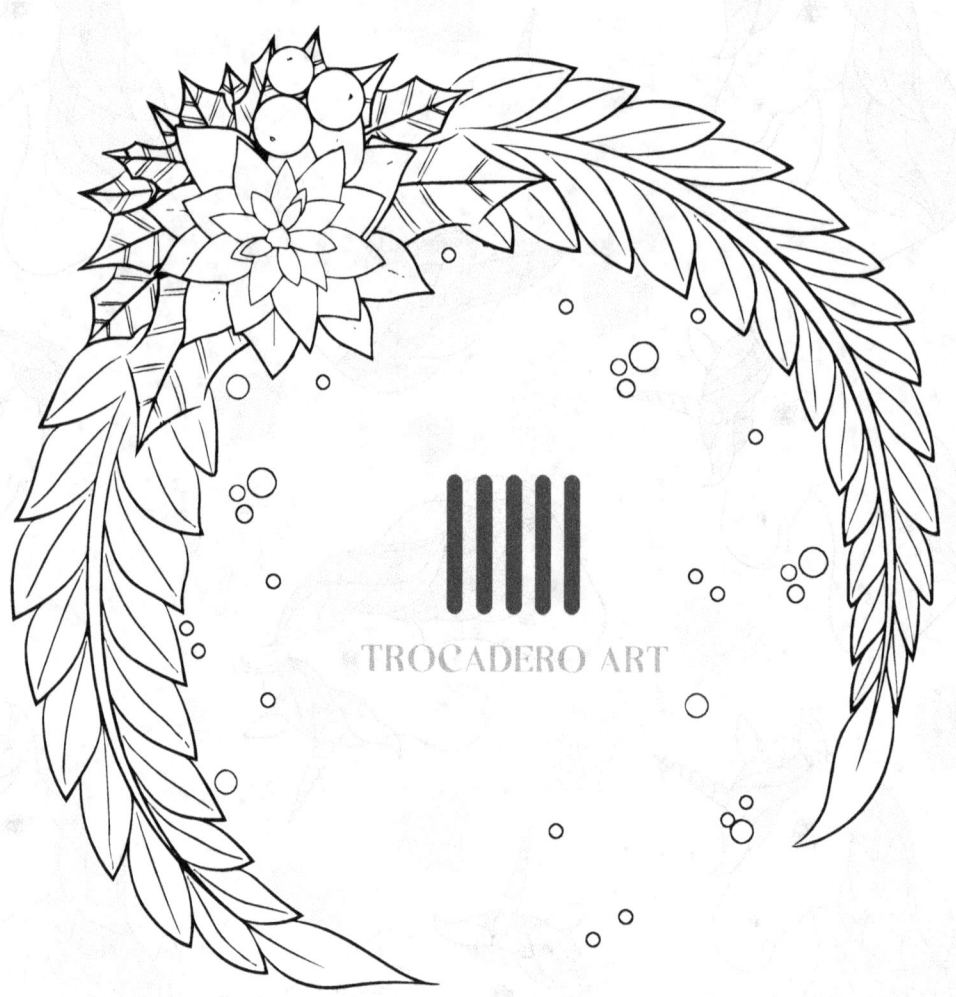

This Book Belong To

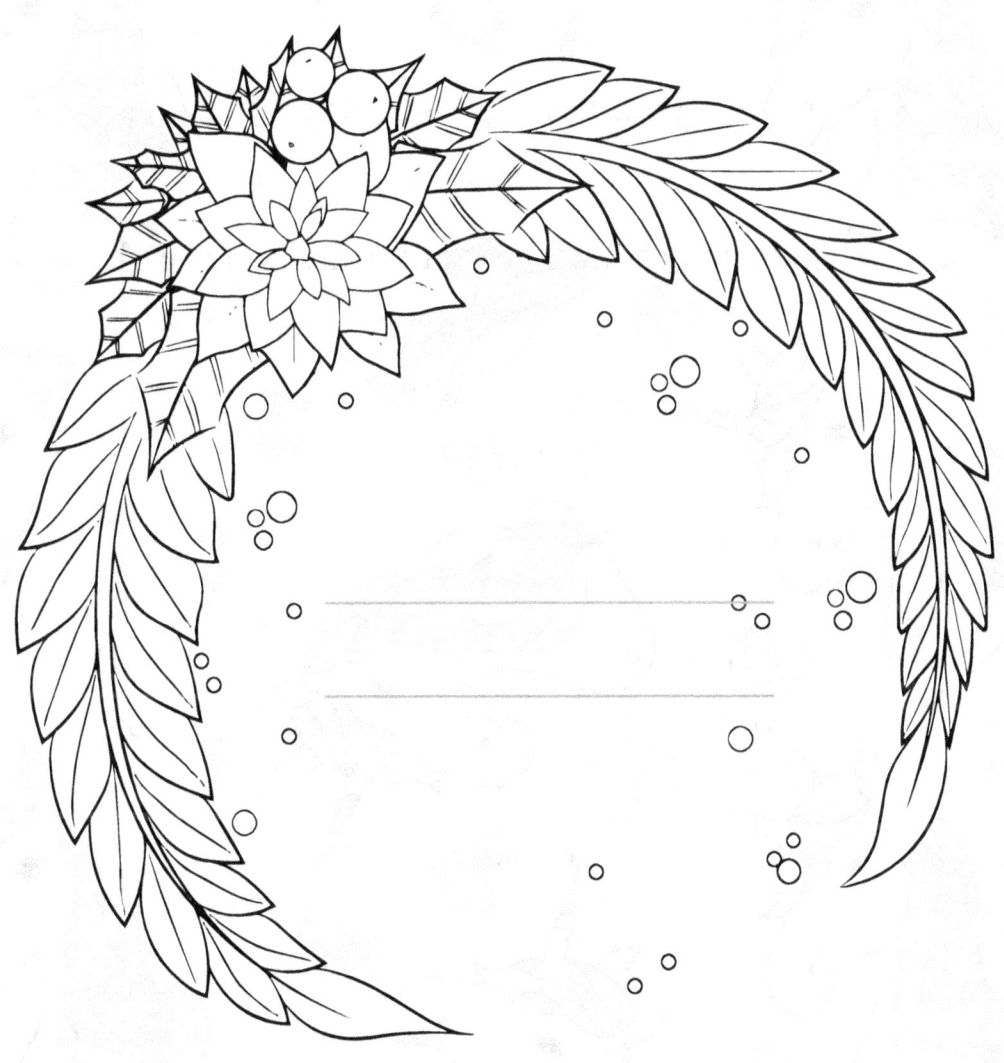

Thank you for supporting

TROCADERO ART

I aim to make sure my customers have the most enjoyable and relaxing coloring experience possible, and I would love to hear your feedback!
Please leave a review on Amazon.

This coloring book has been created with this manner, which is an excellent way for your kids to raise the creativity in their minds !!

Color Test Page

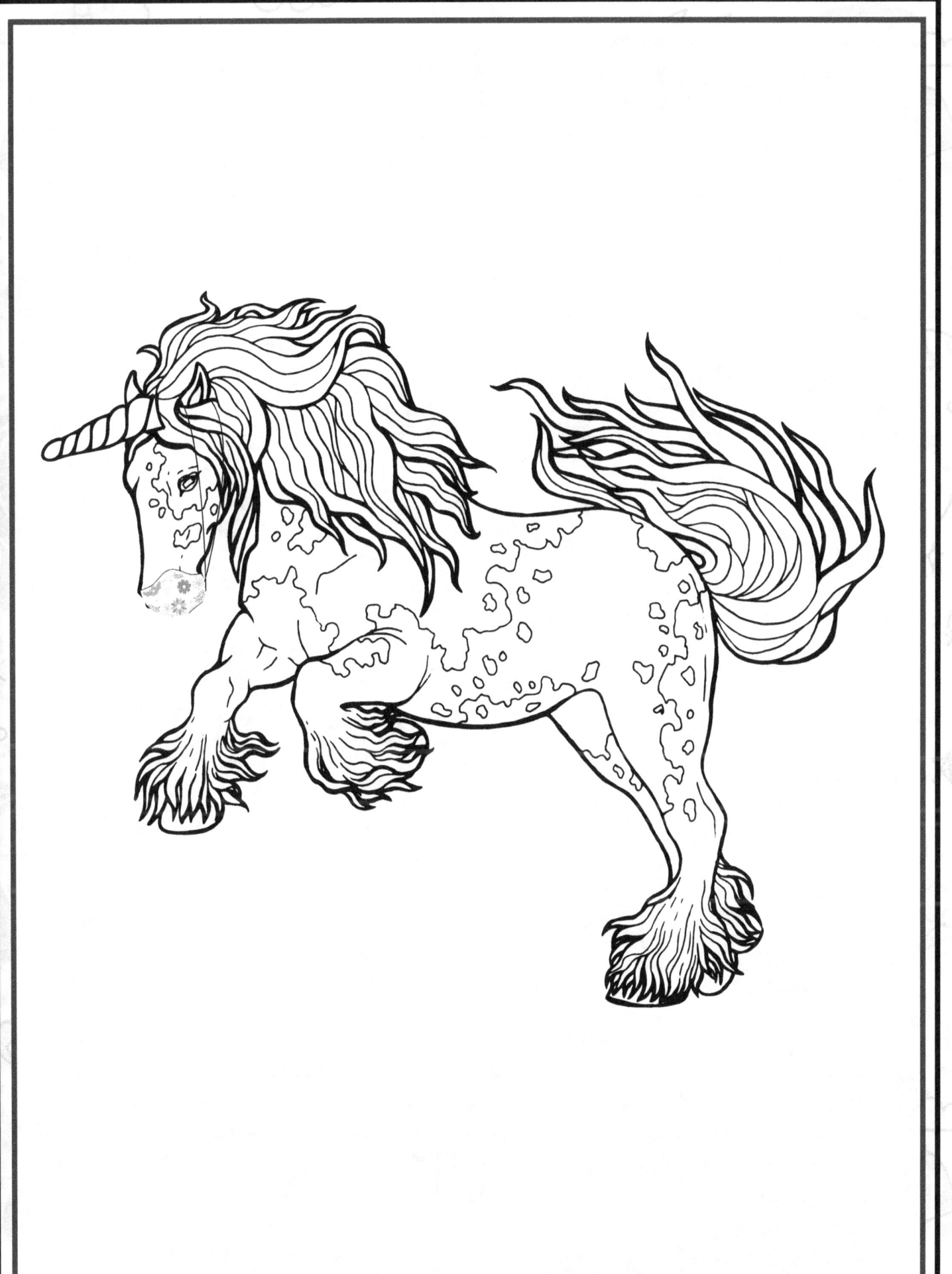

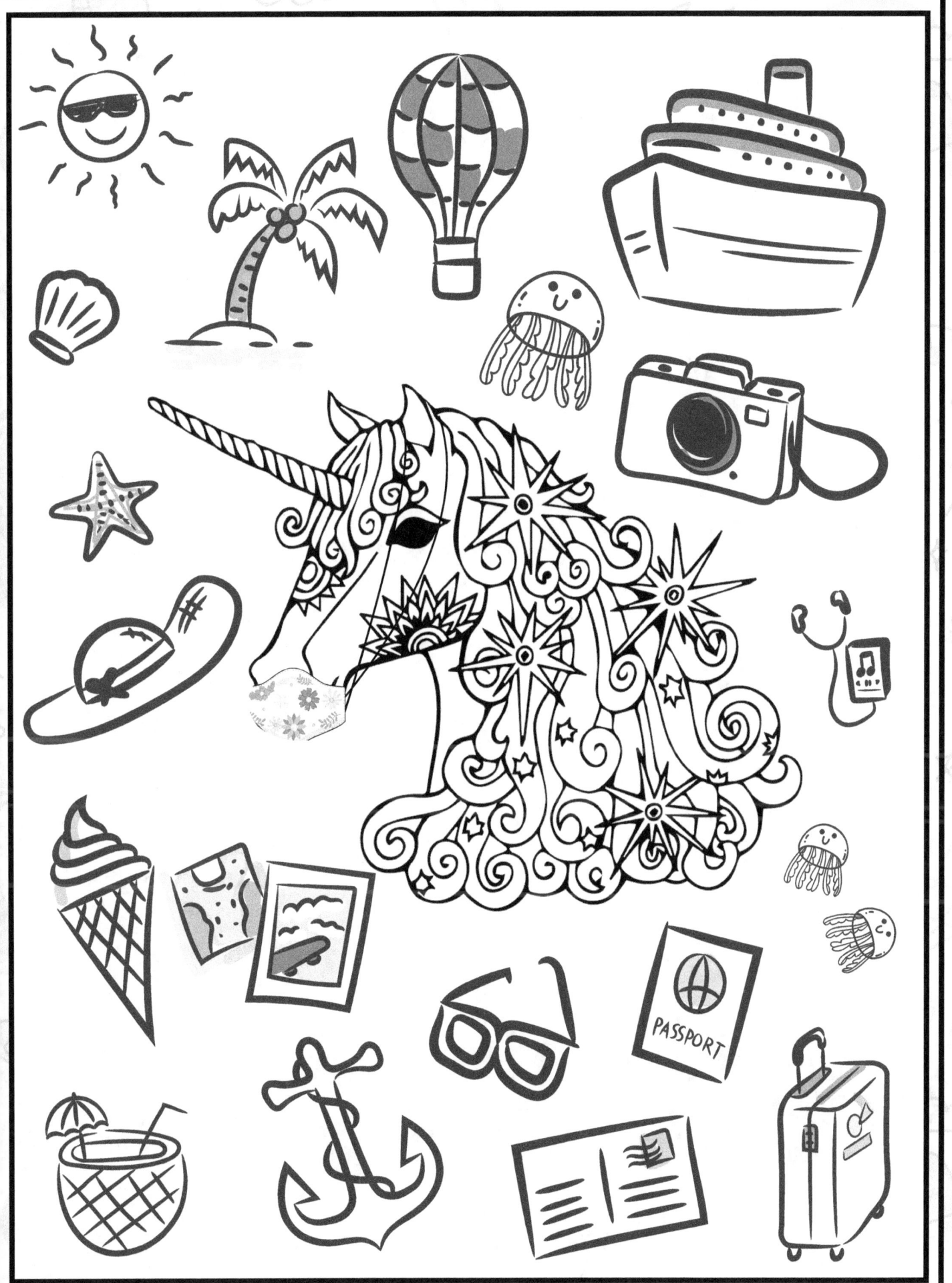

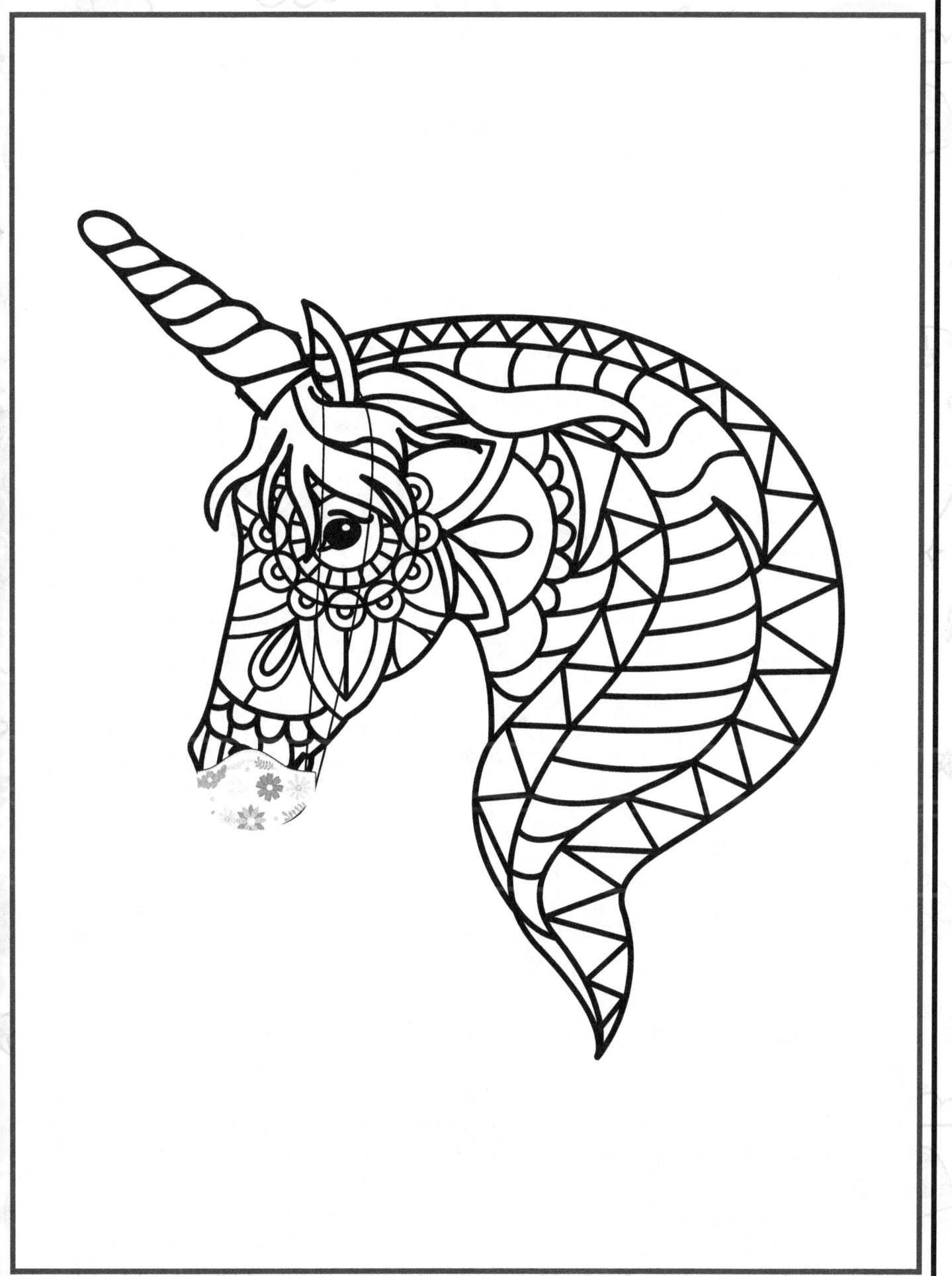

Maze 1

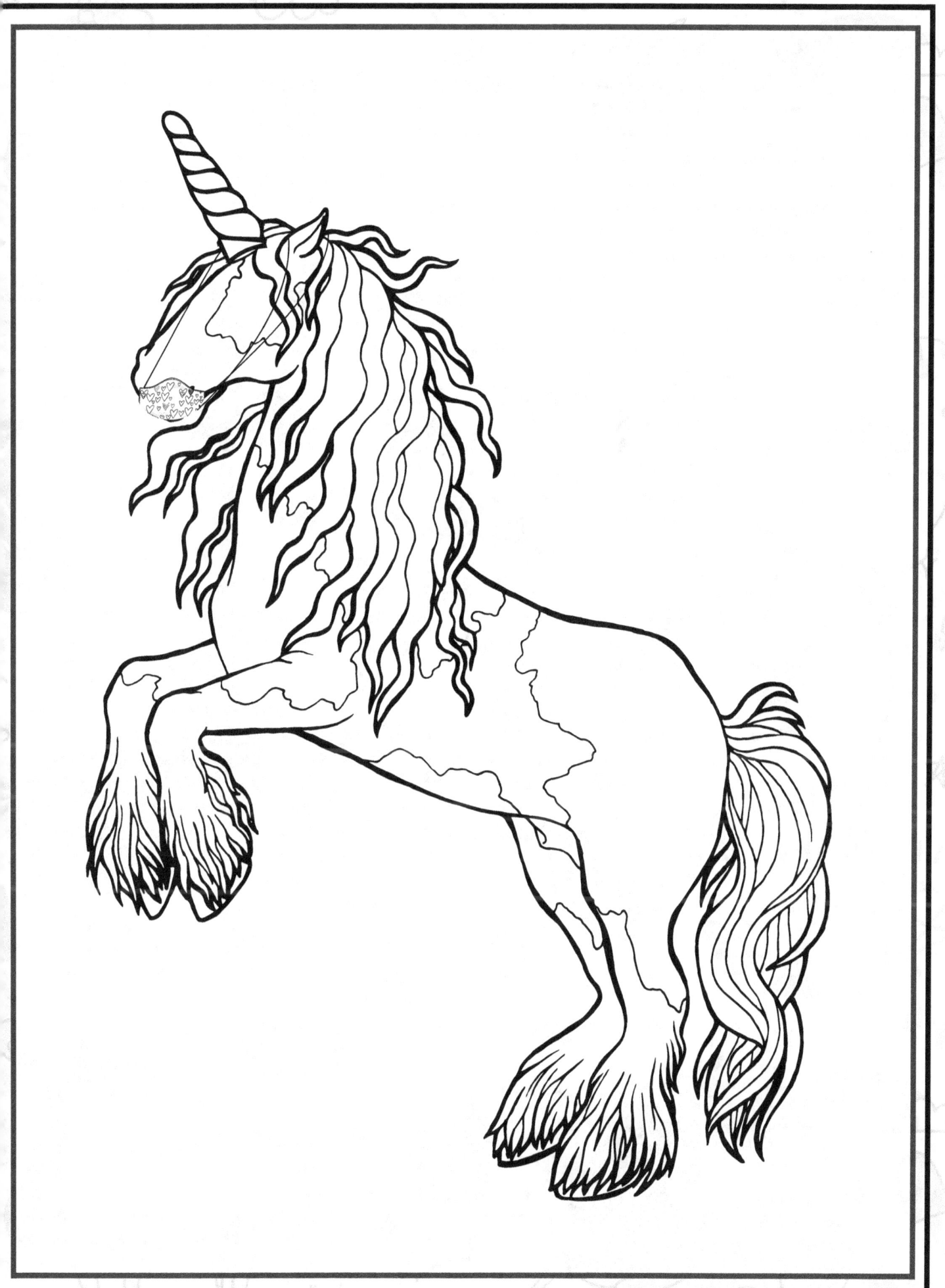

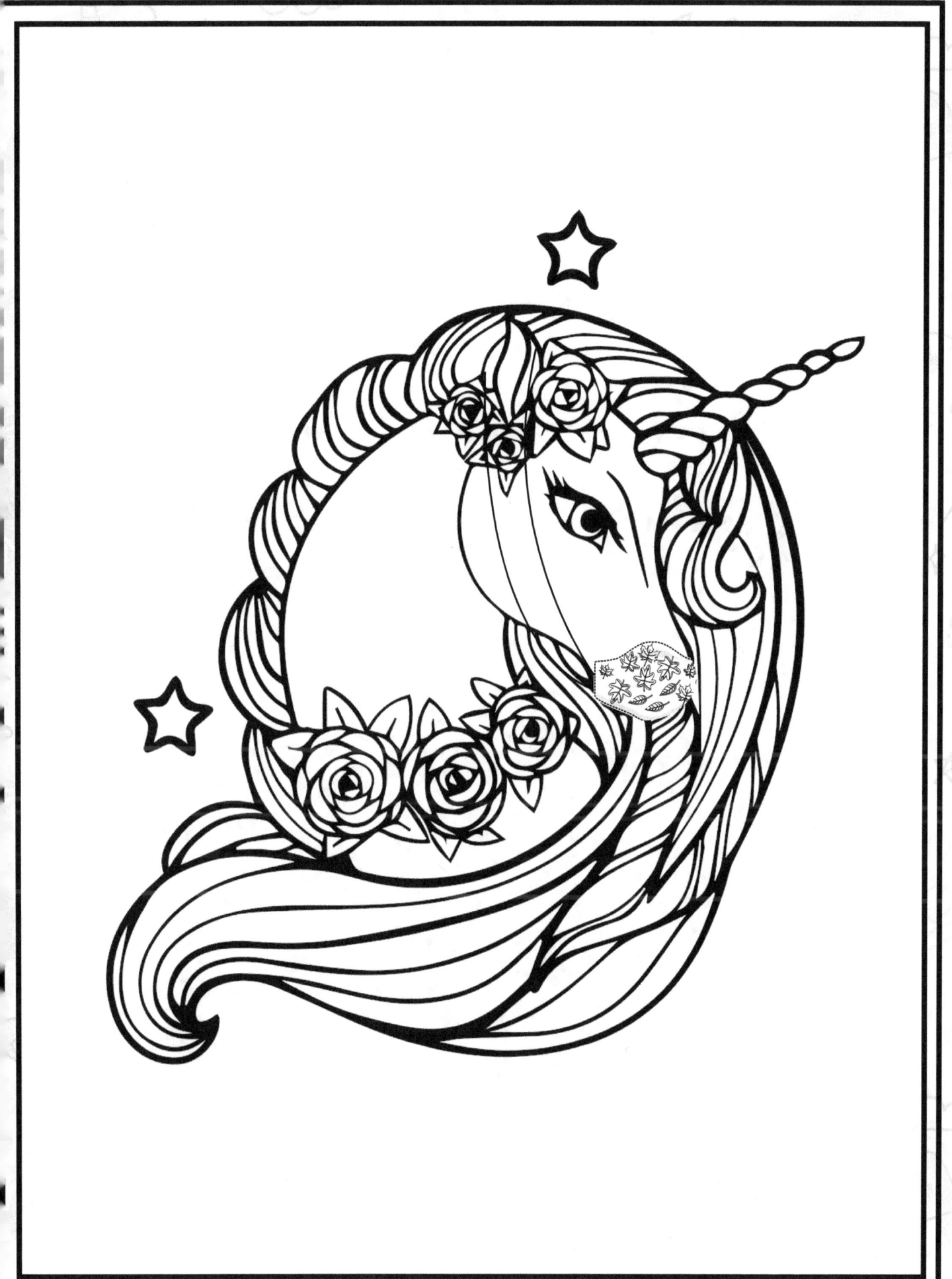

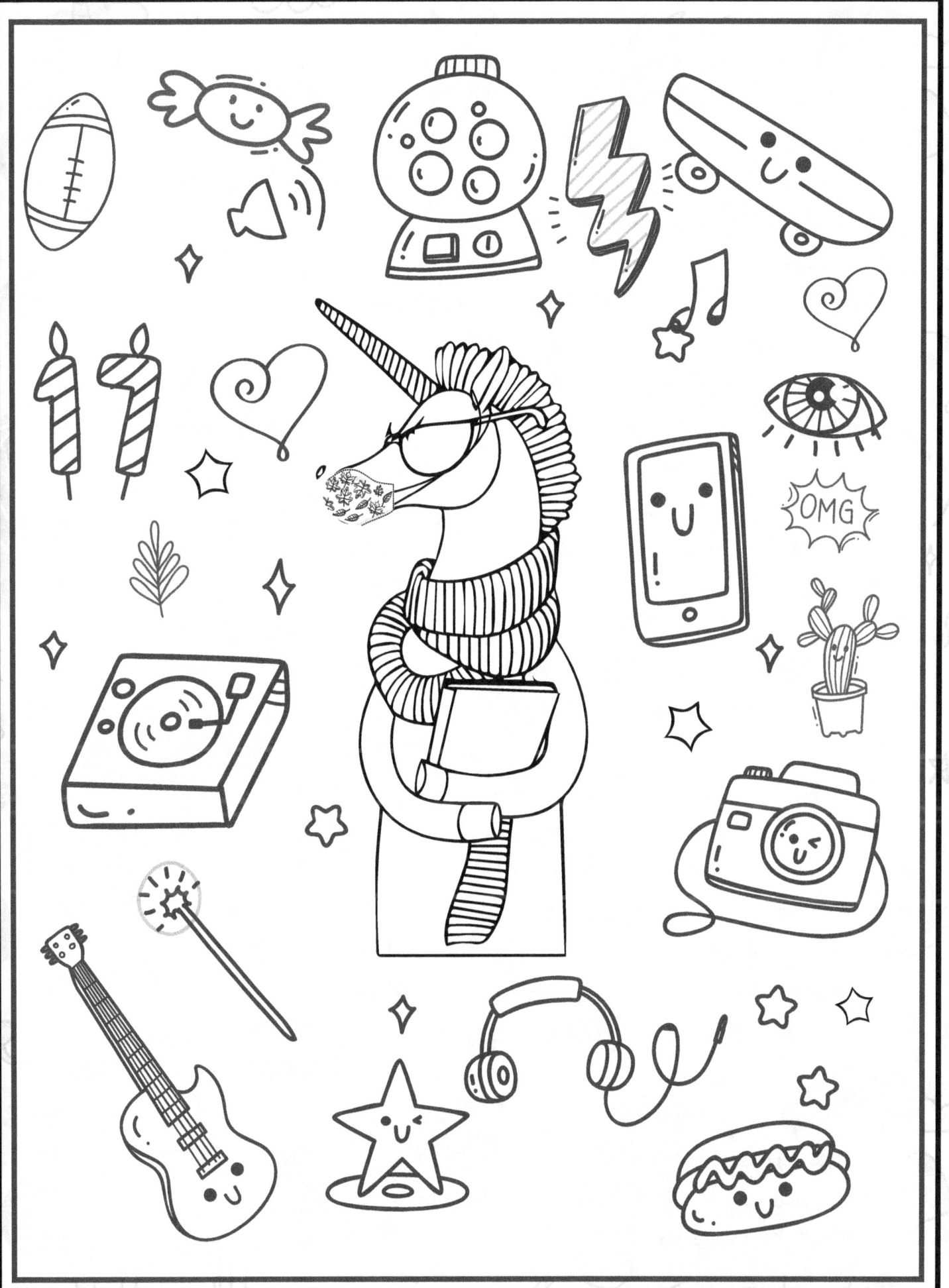

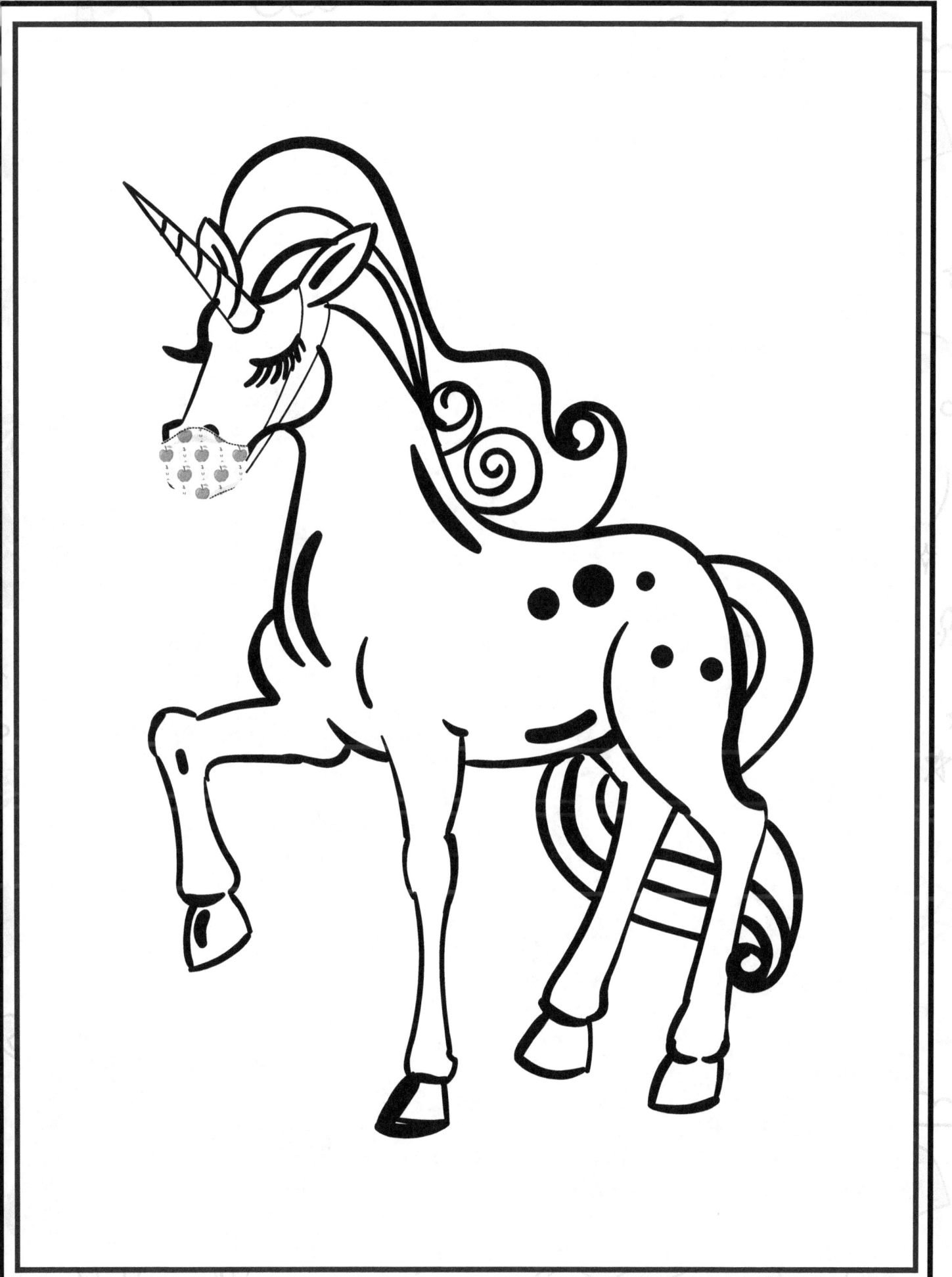

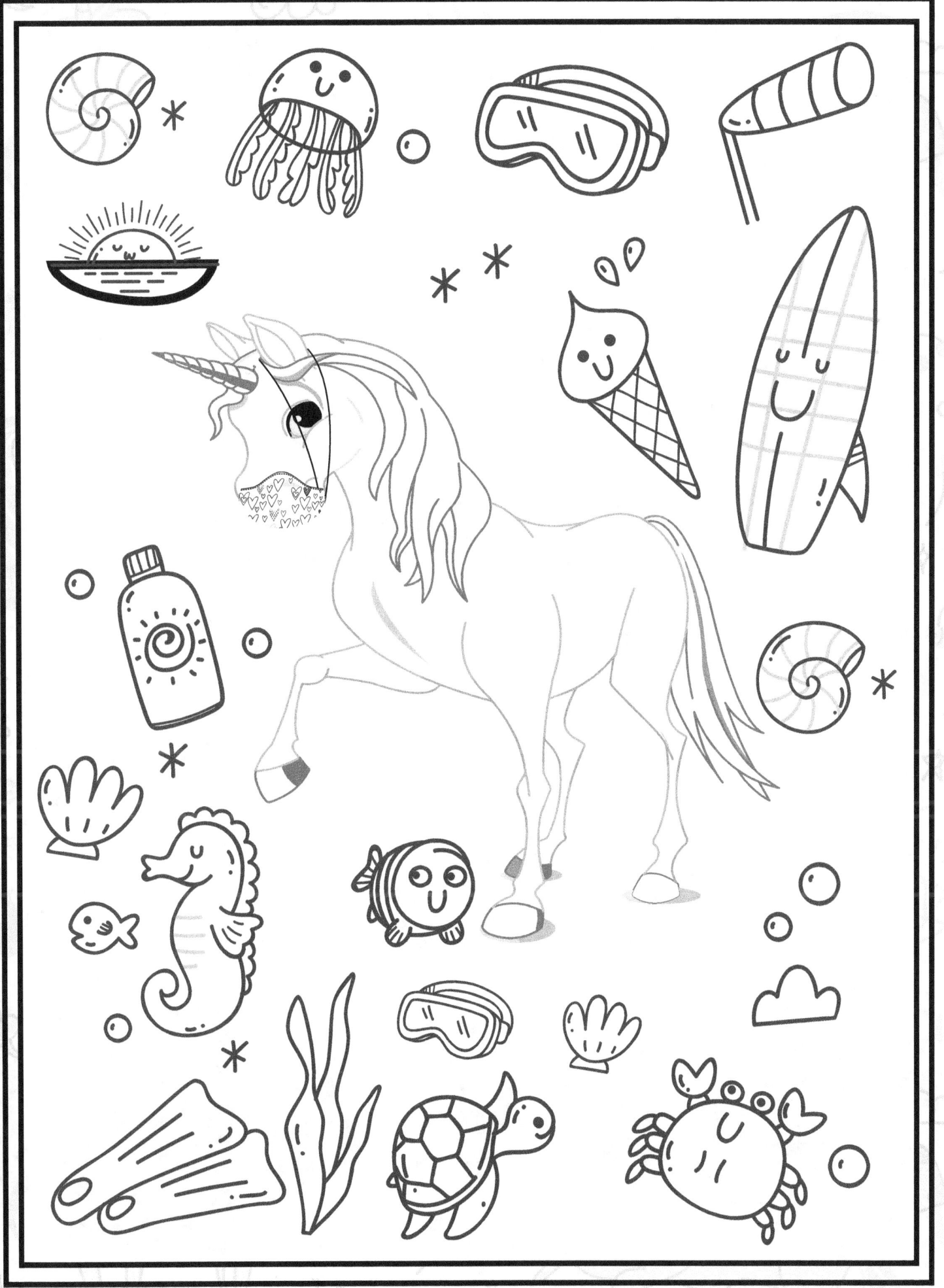

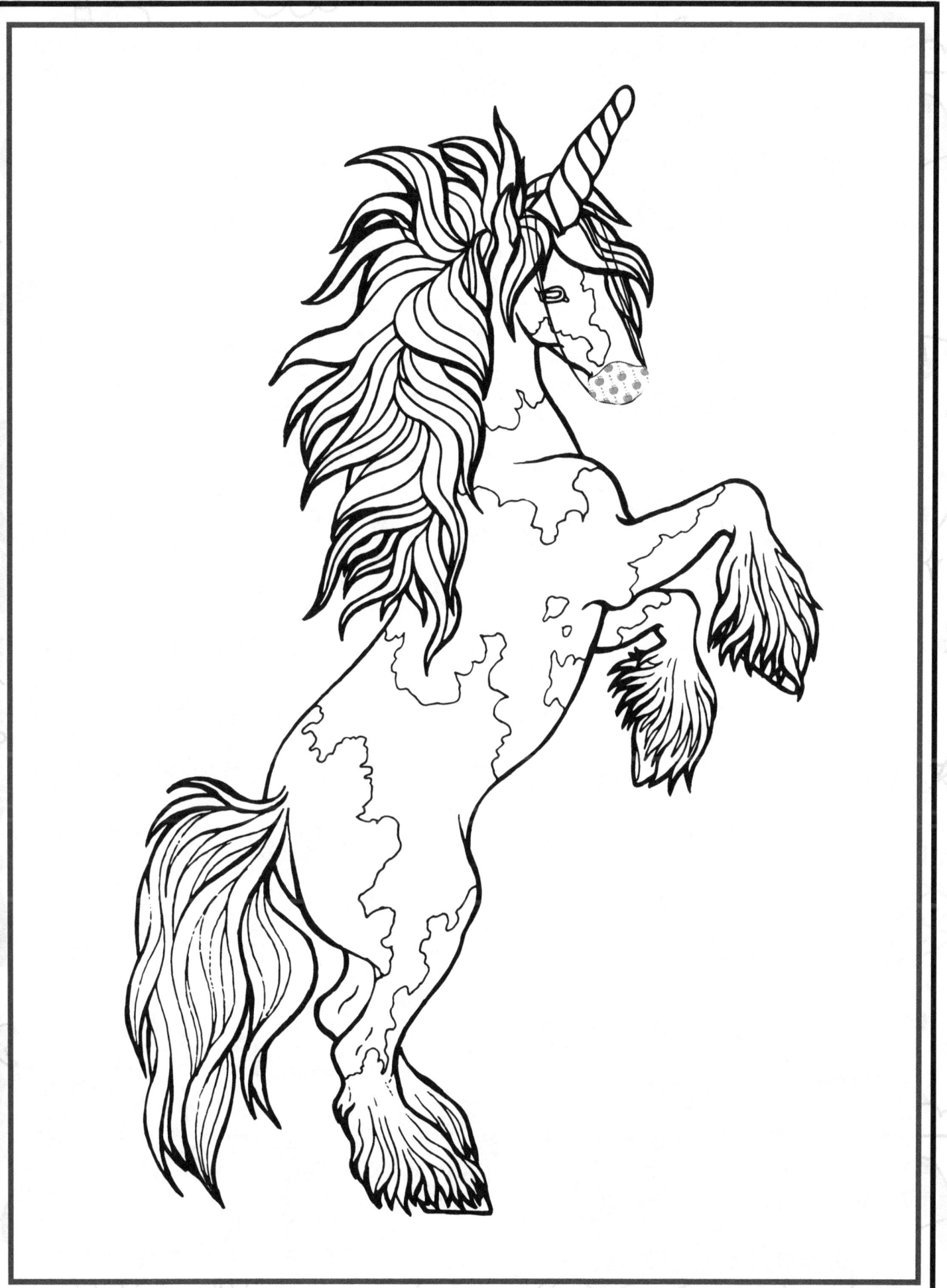

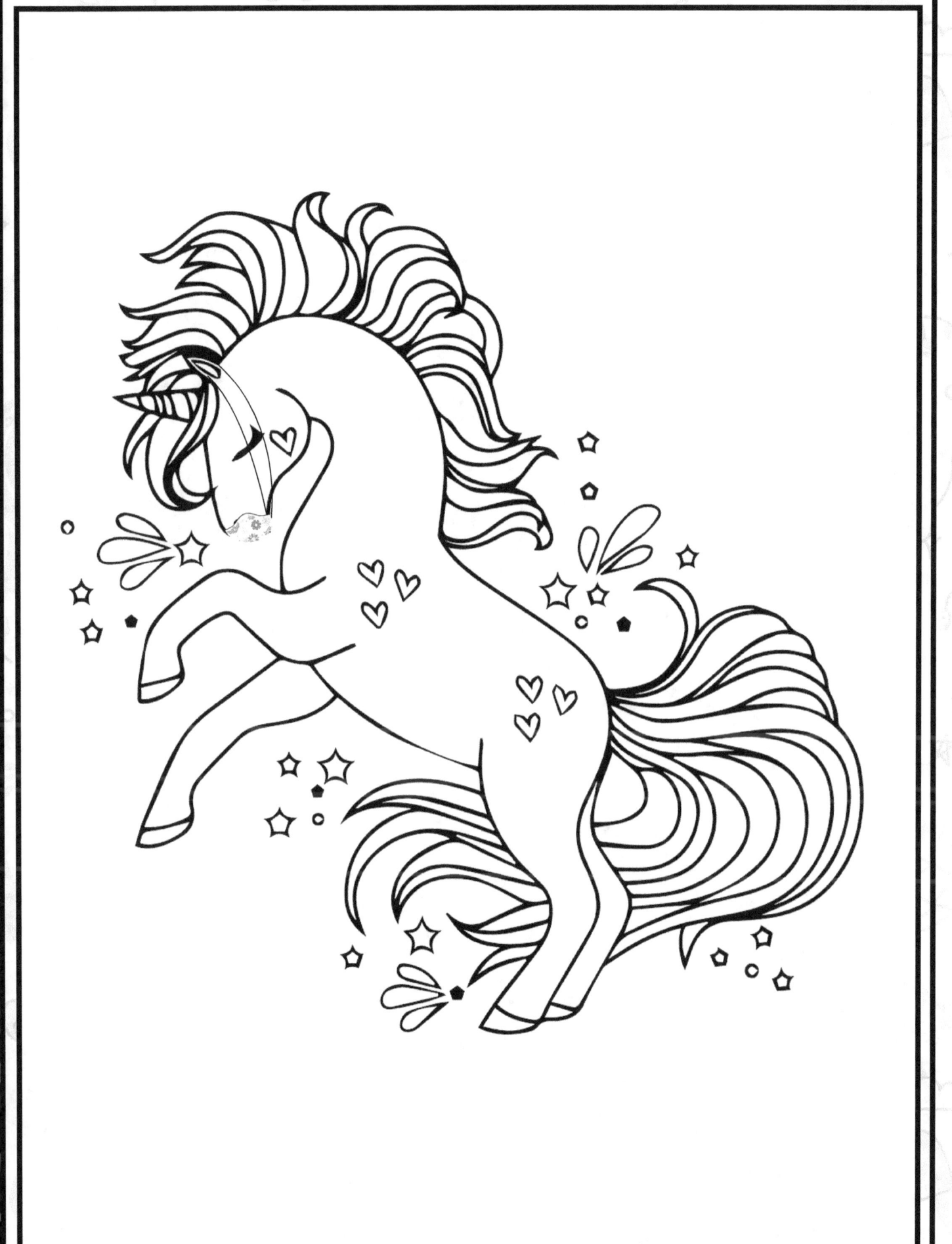

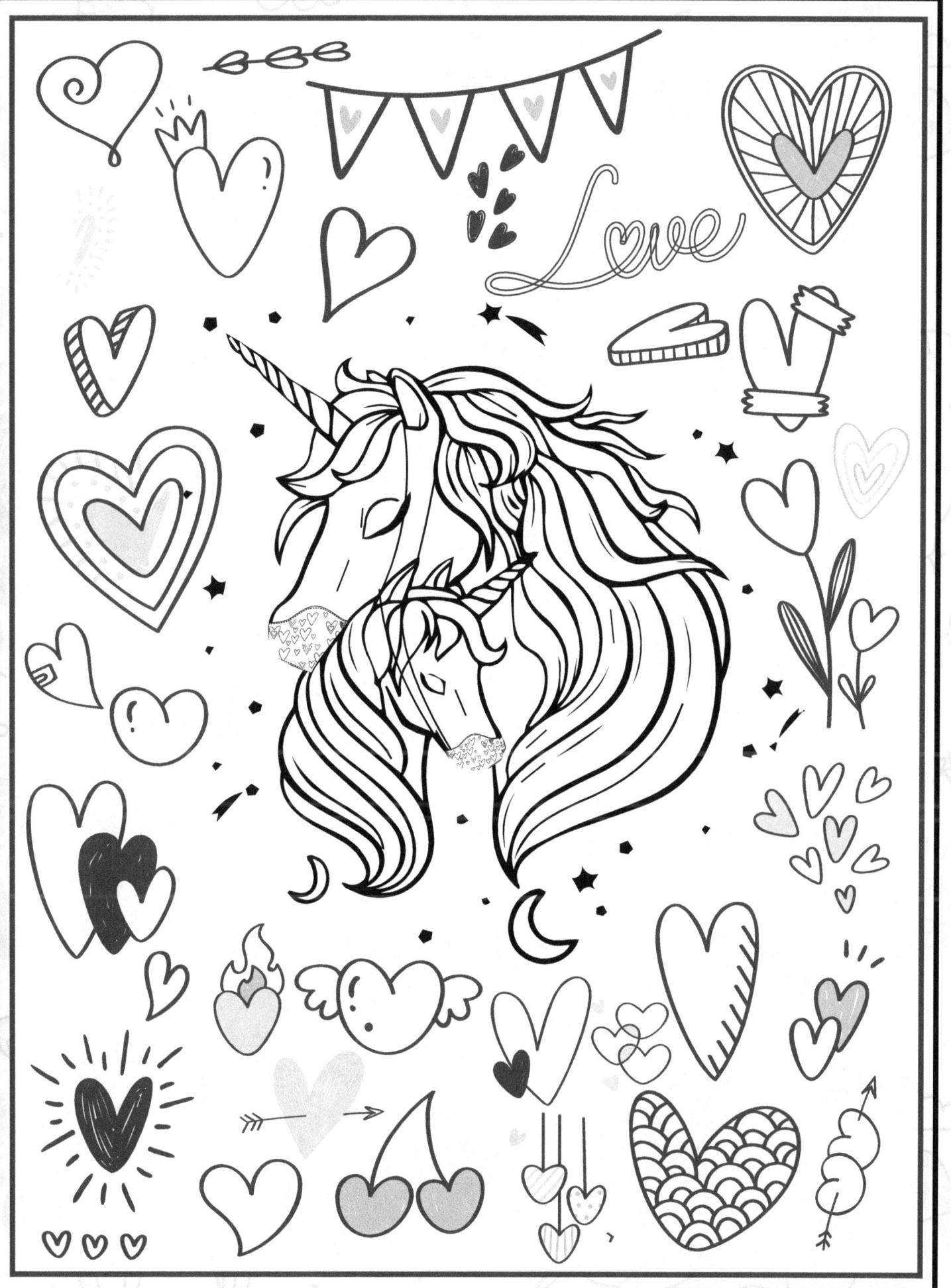

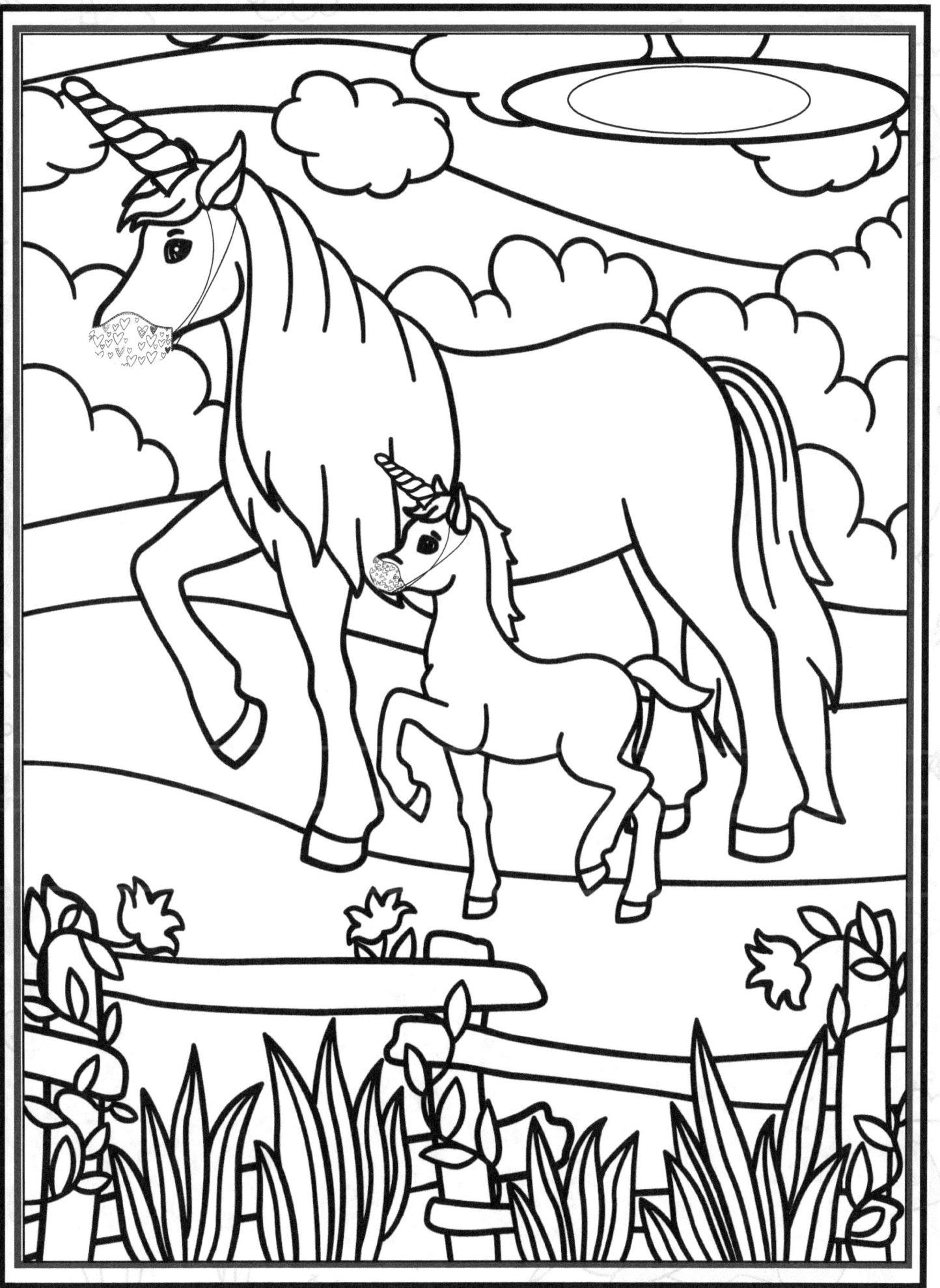

Maze 2

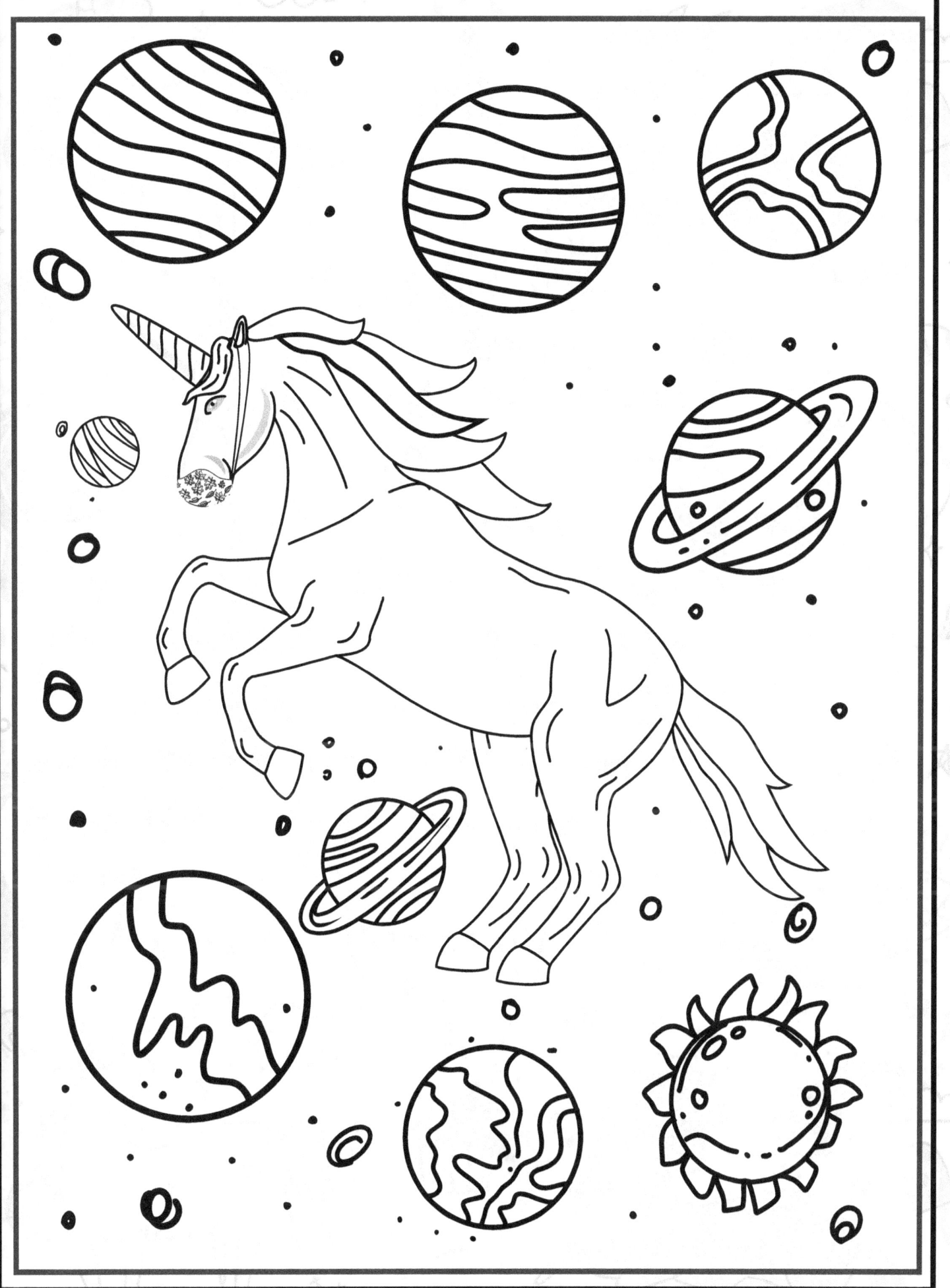

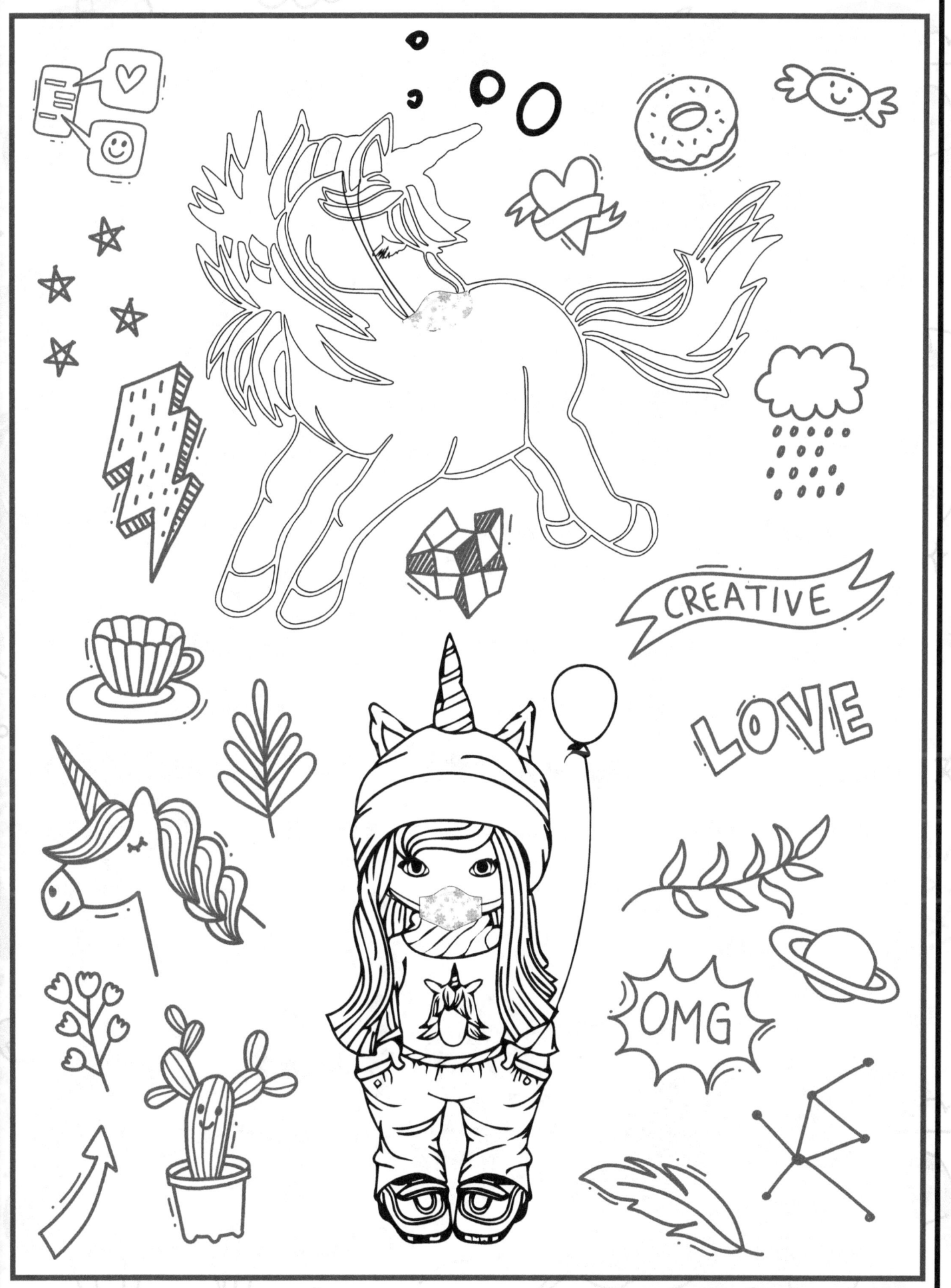

Maze 3

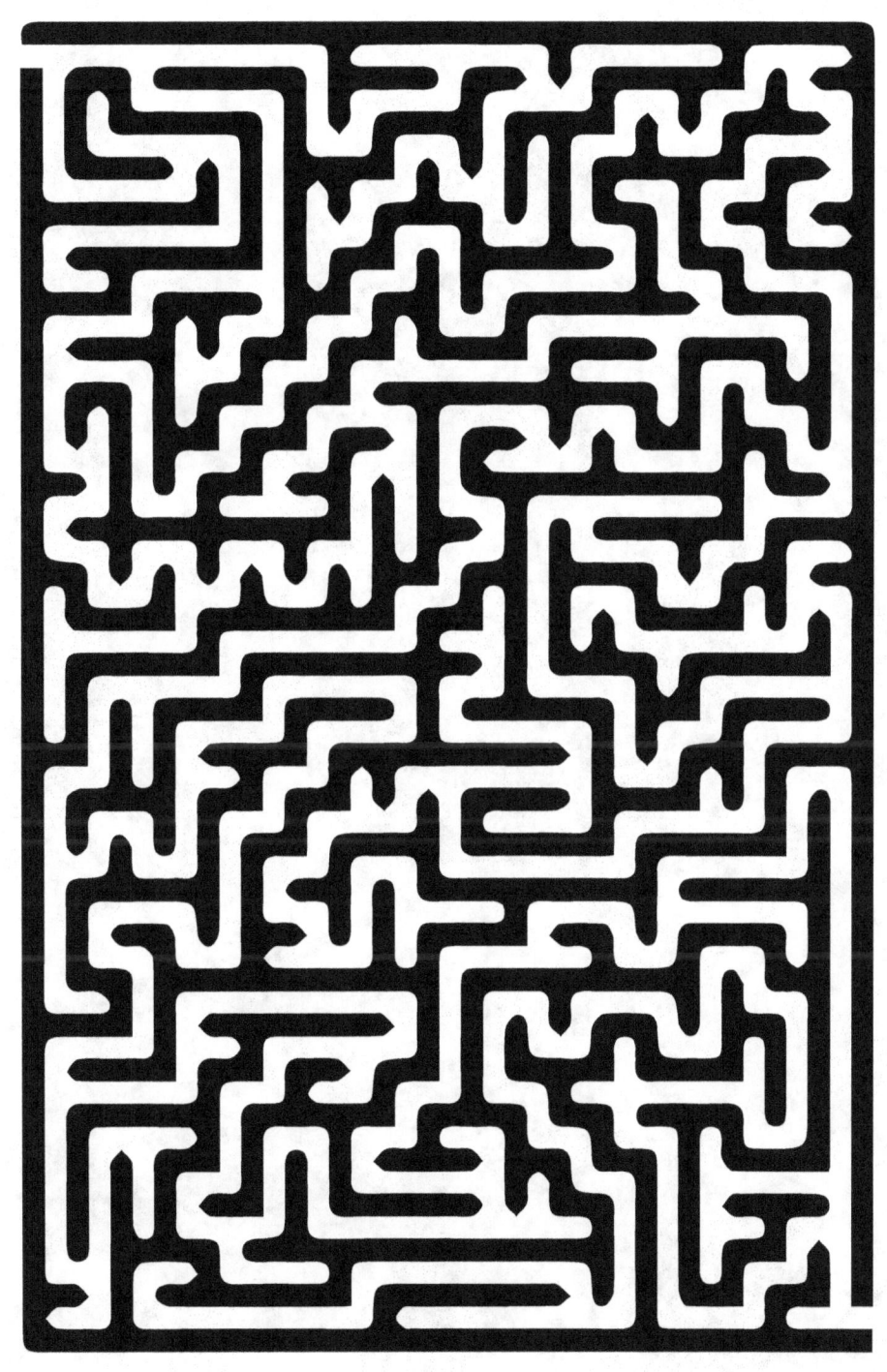

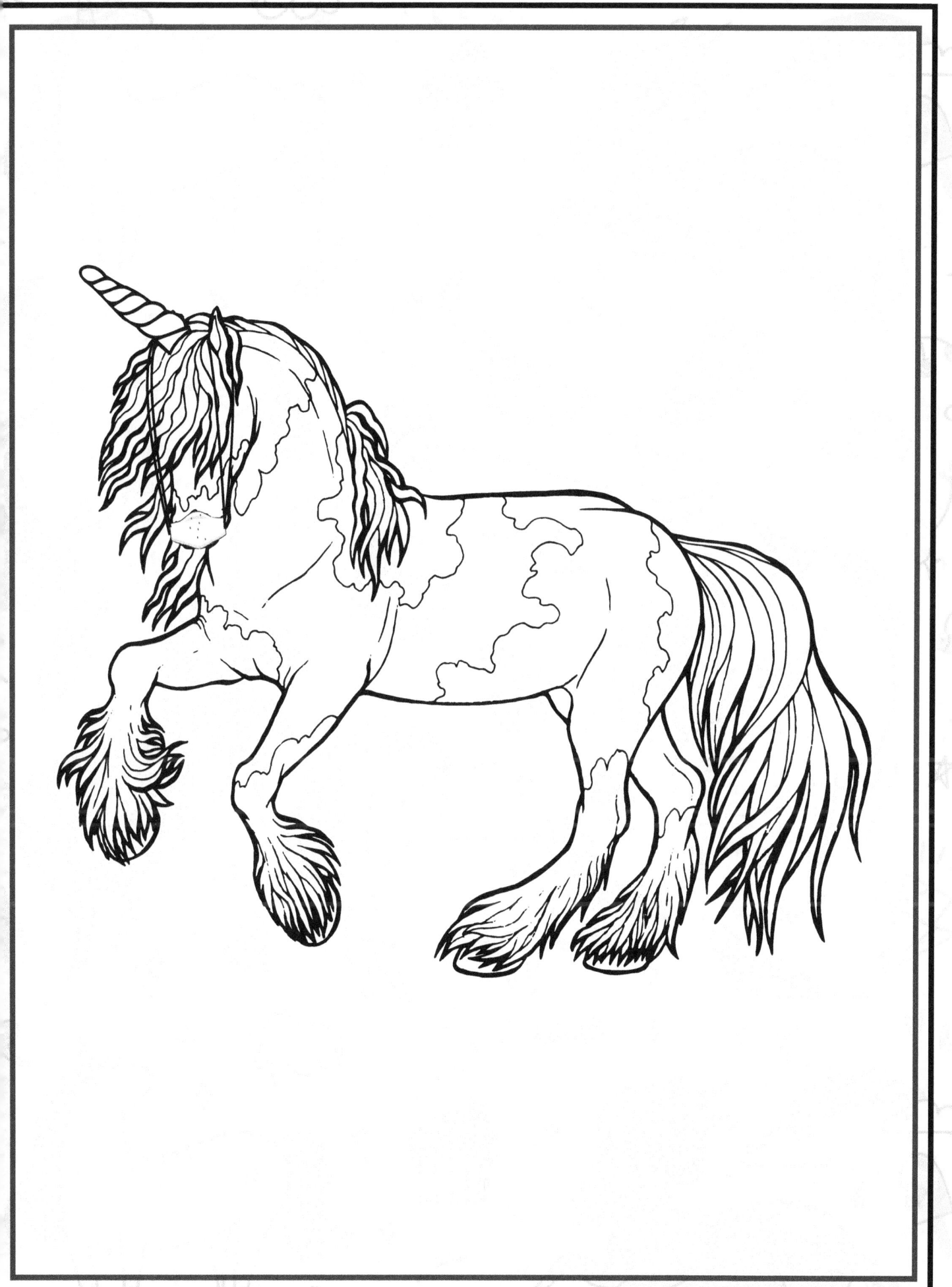

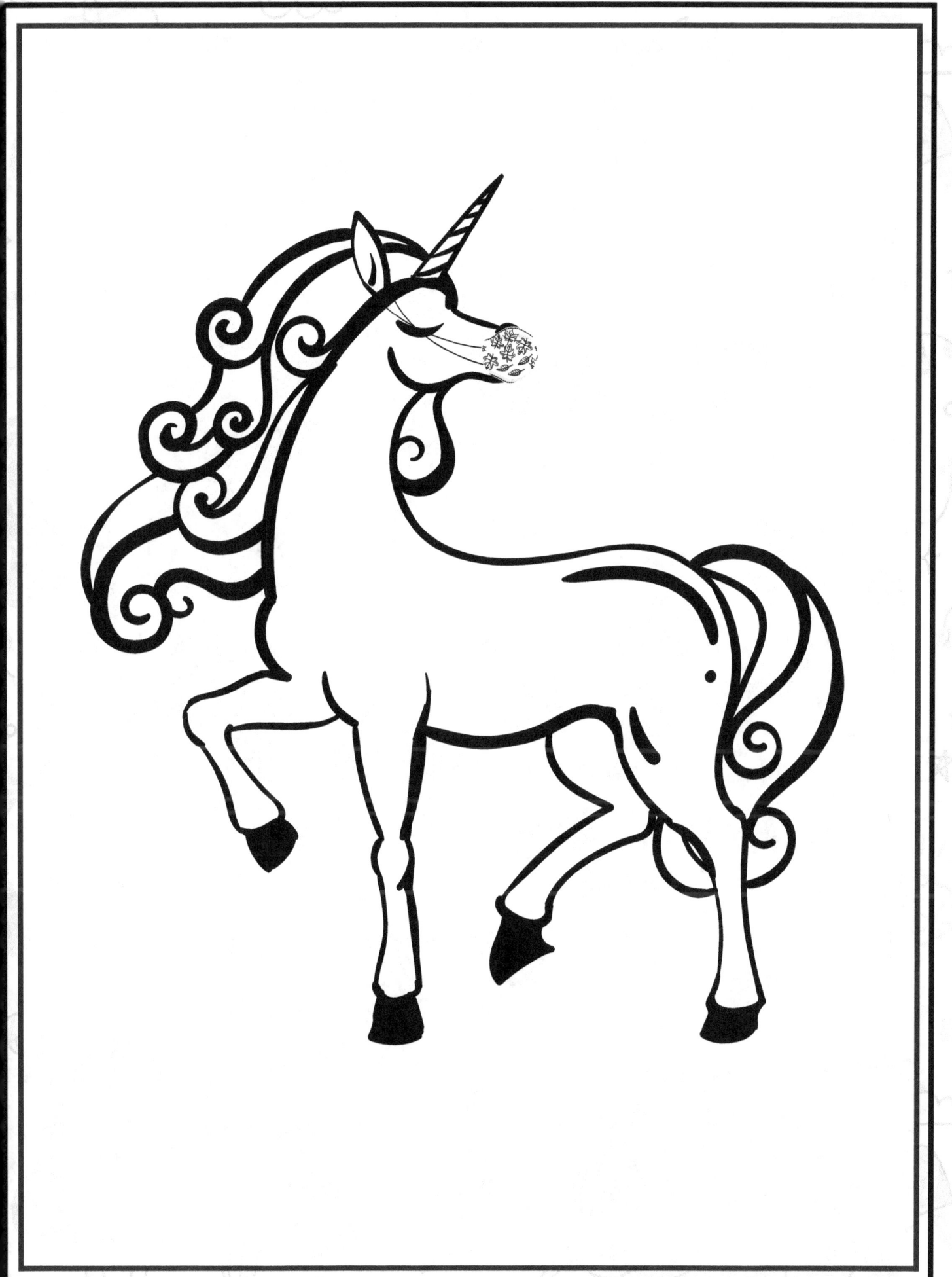

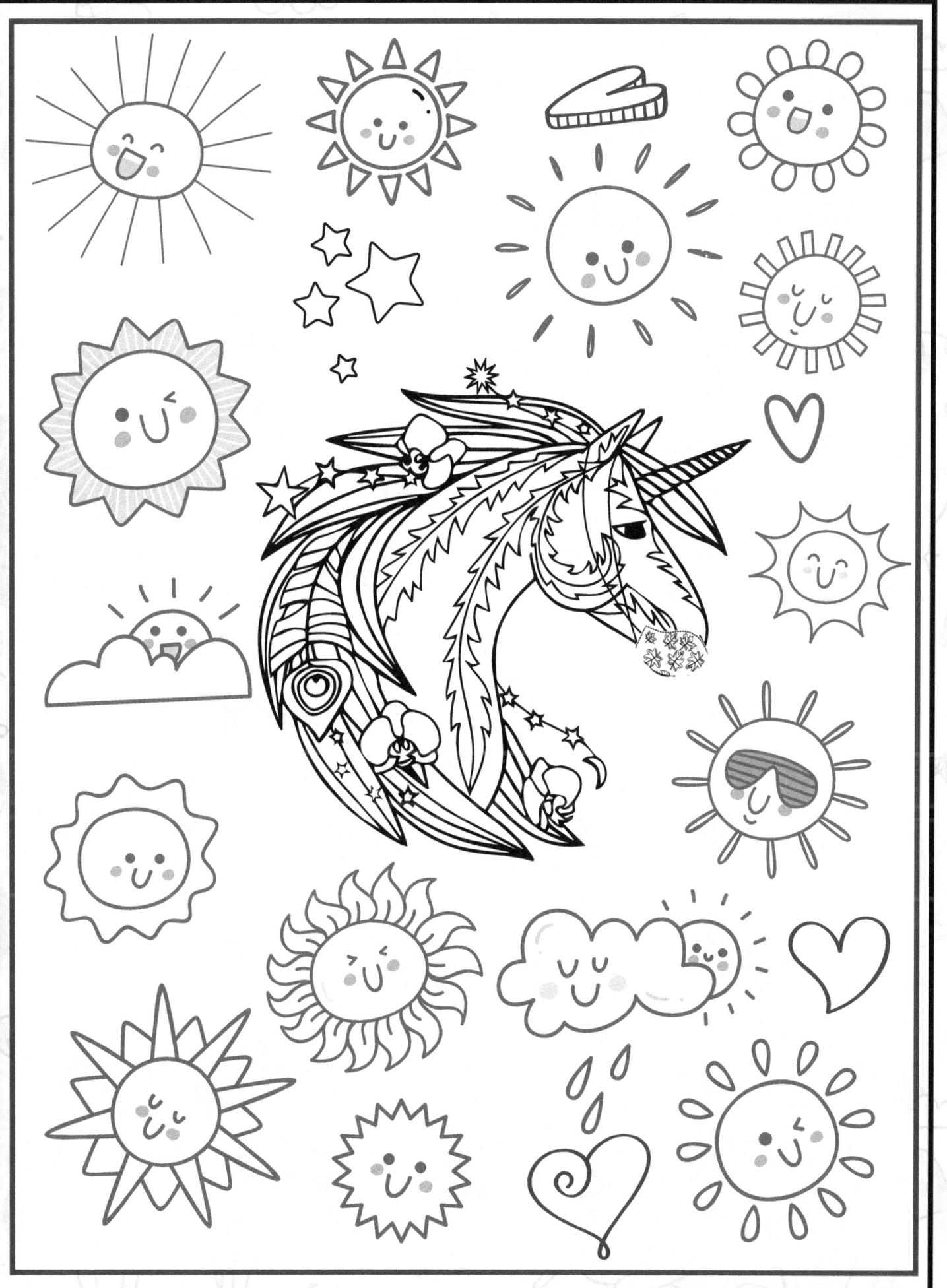

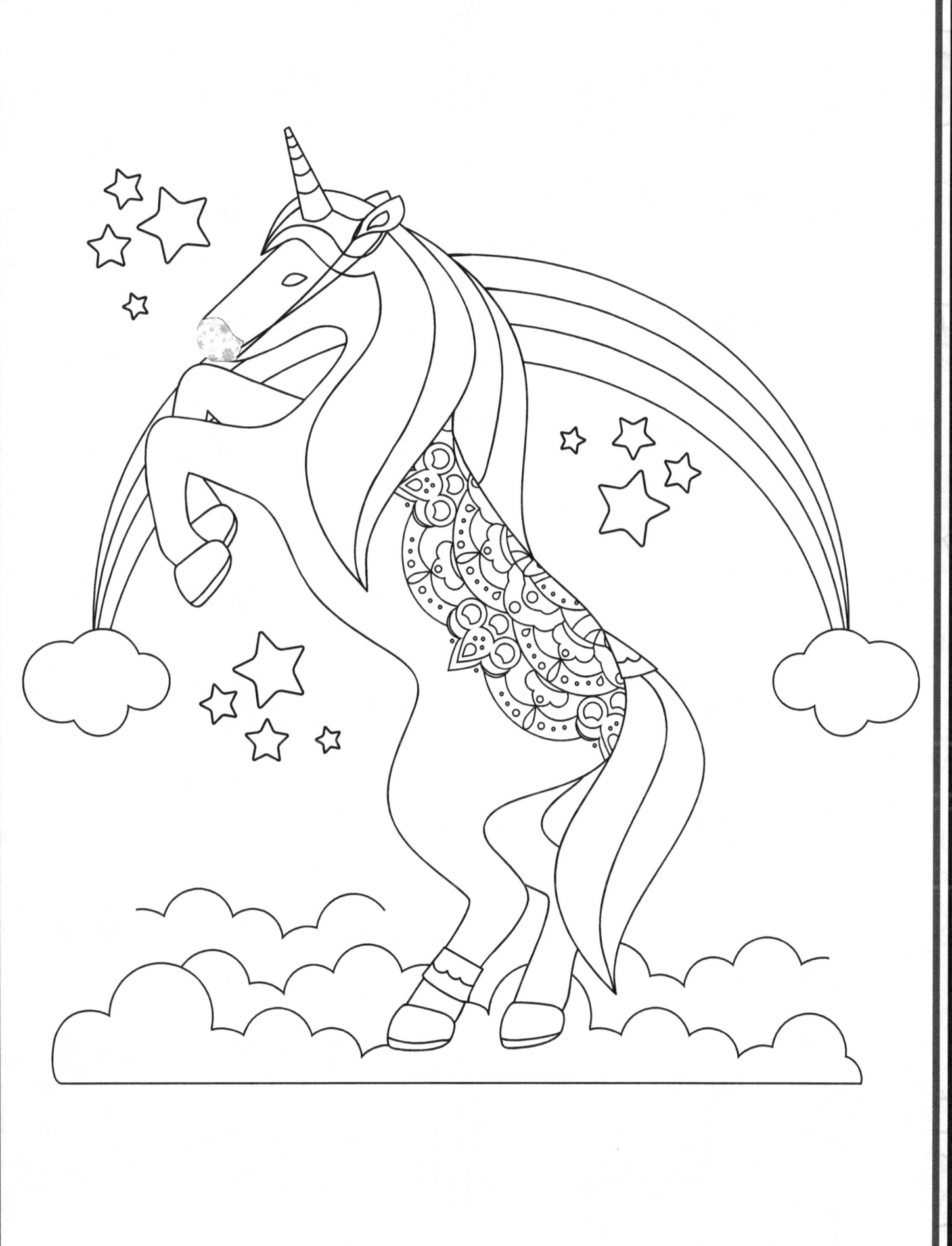

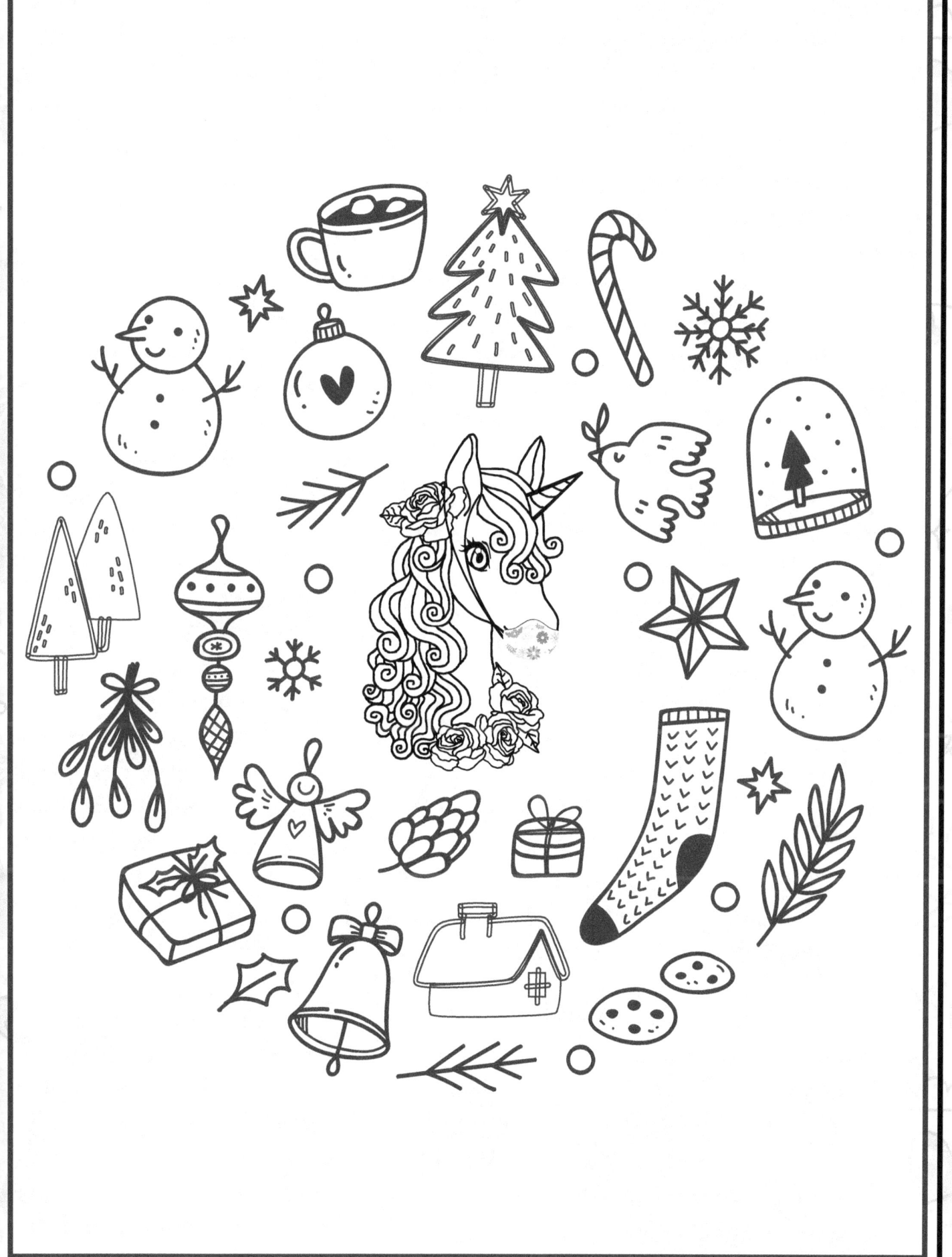

Maze 4

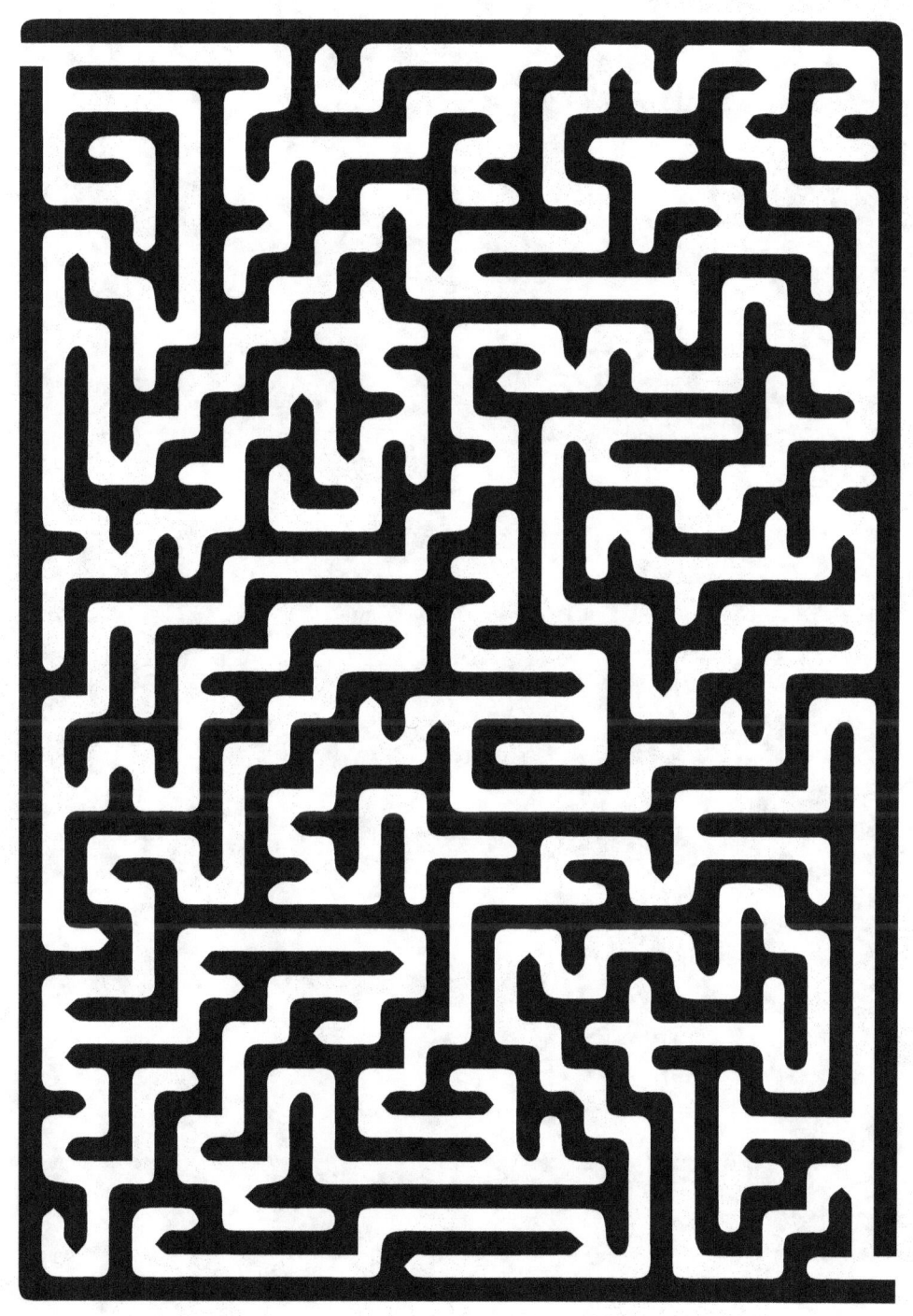

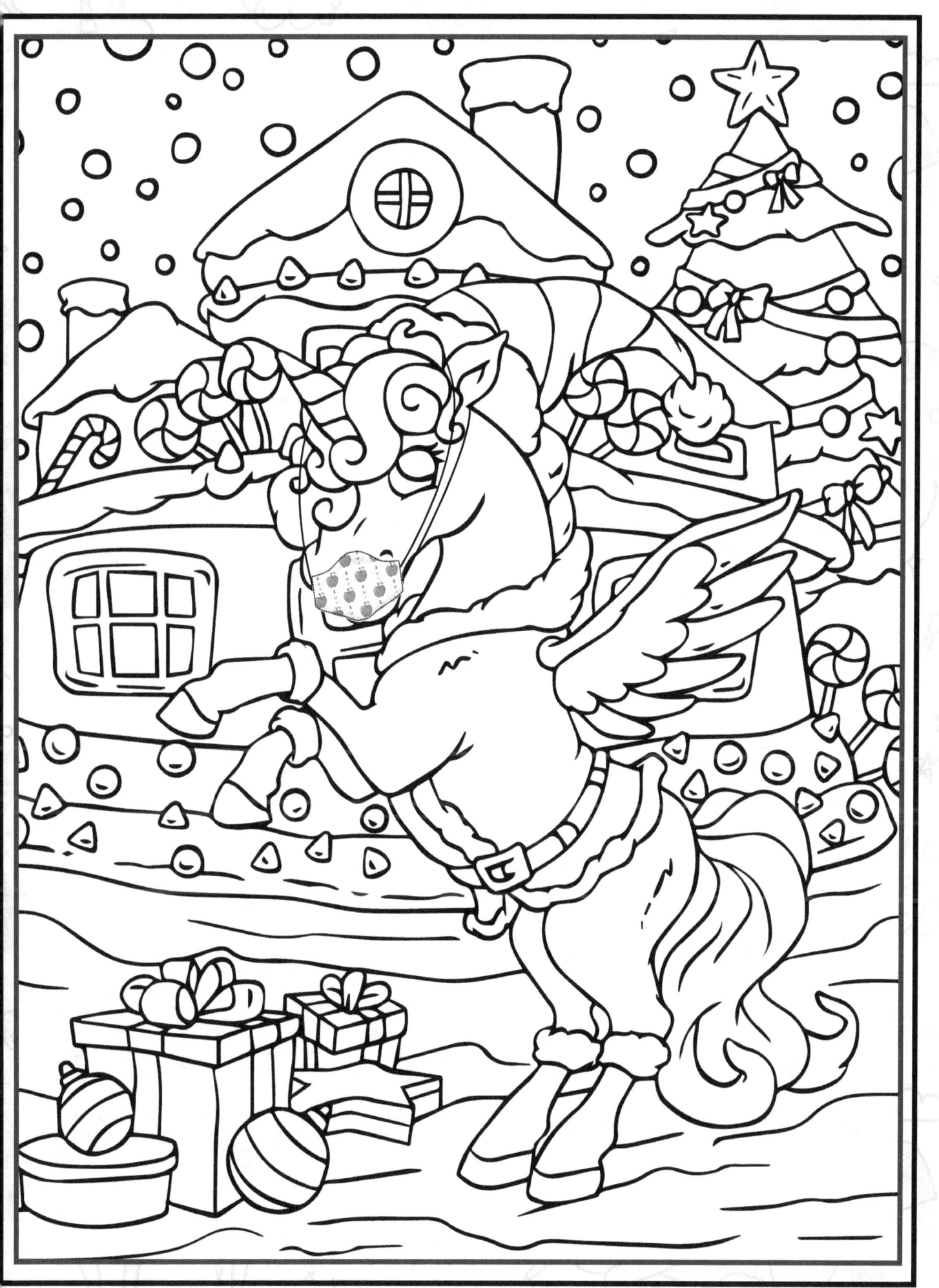

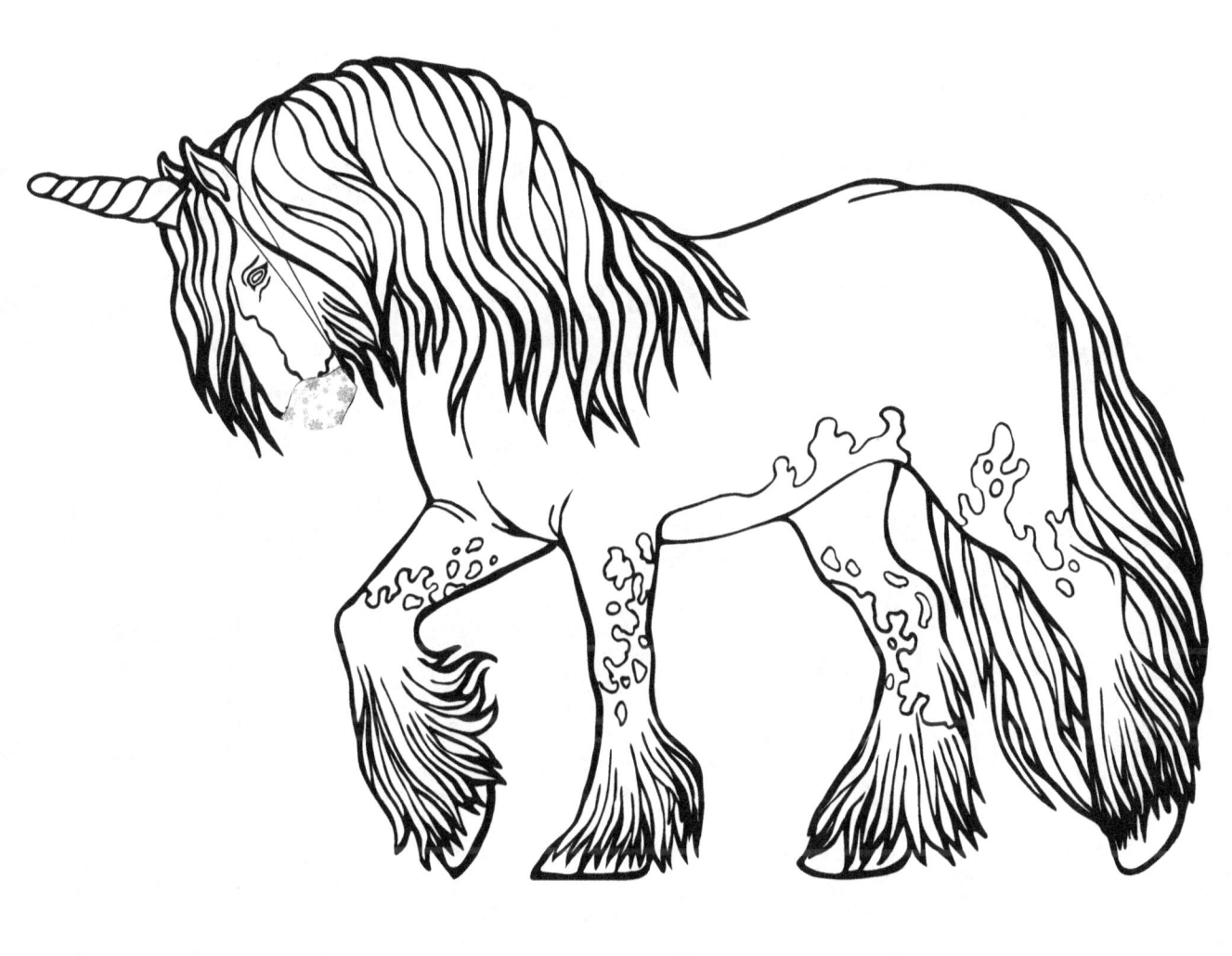

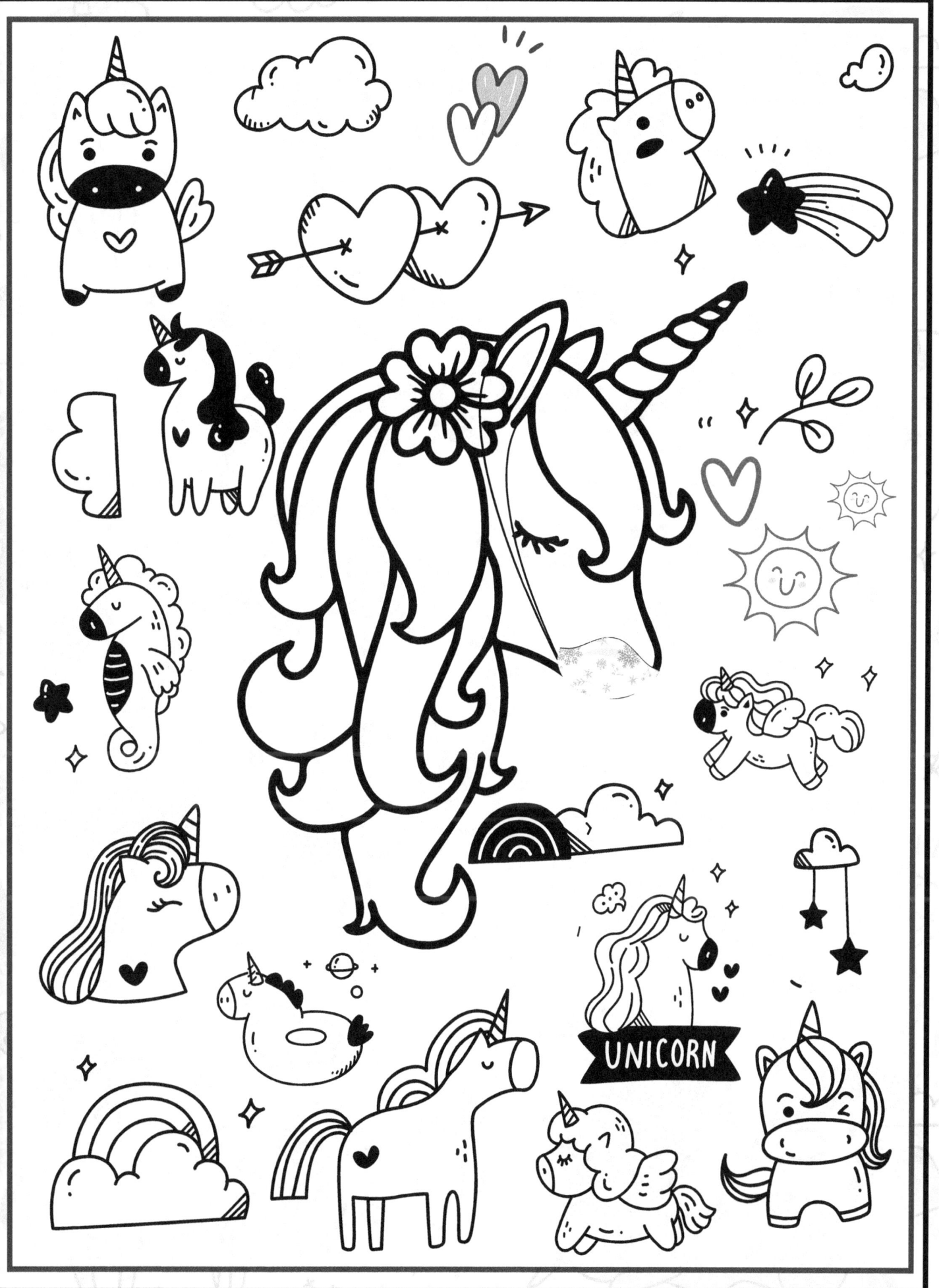

Maze 5

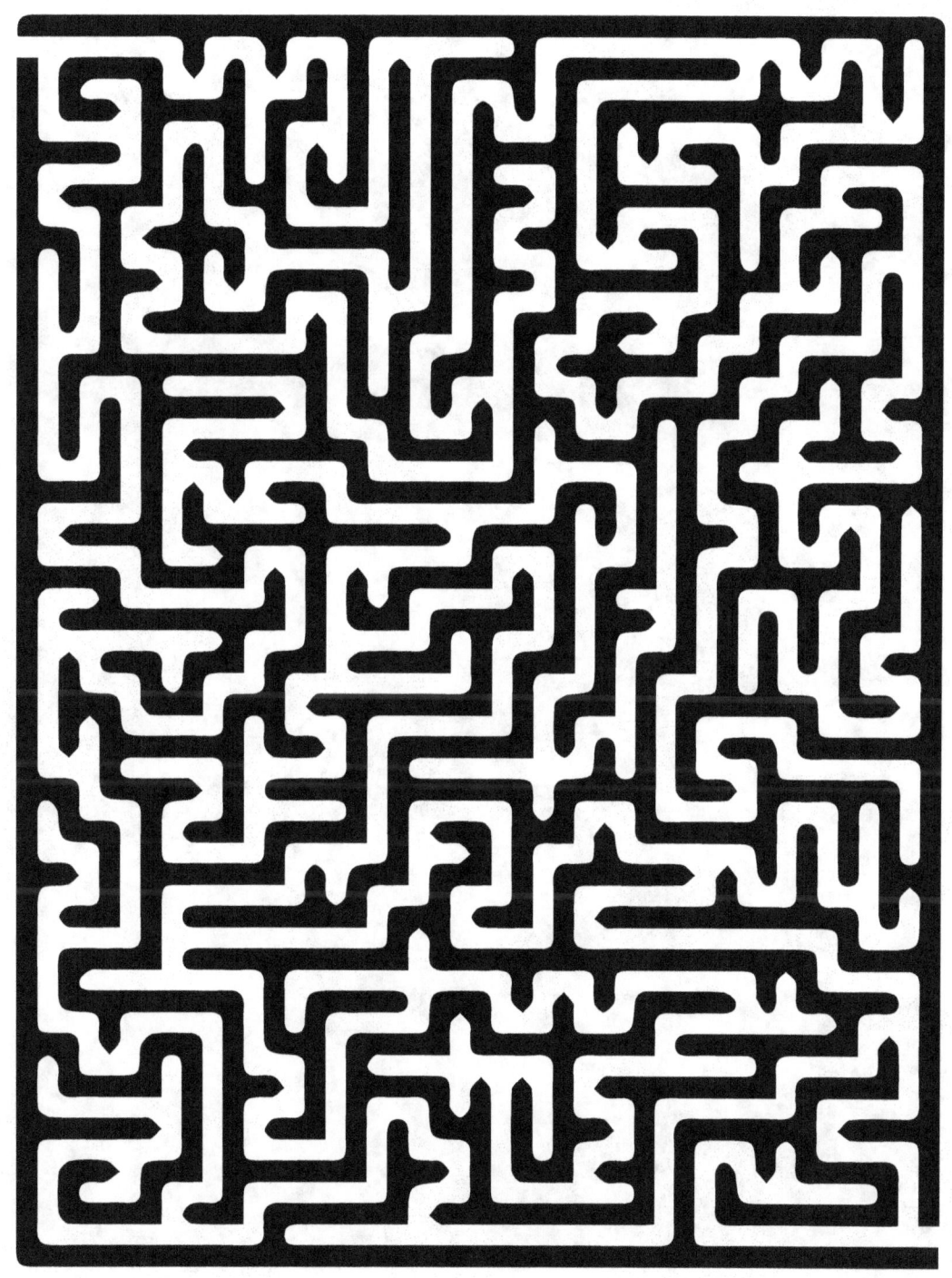

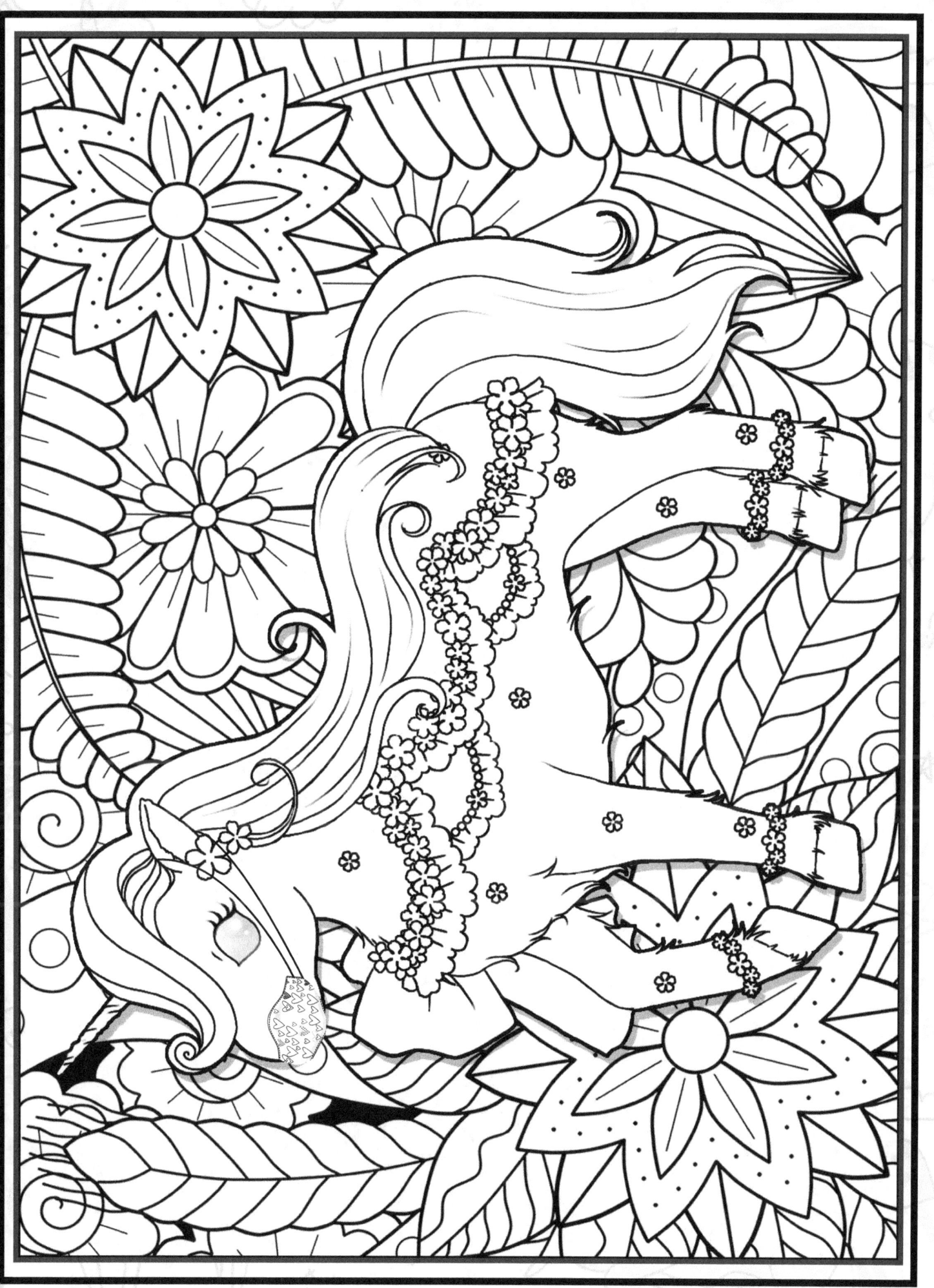

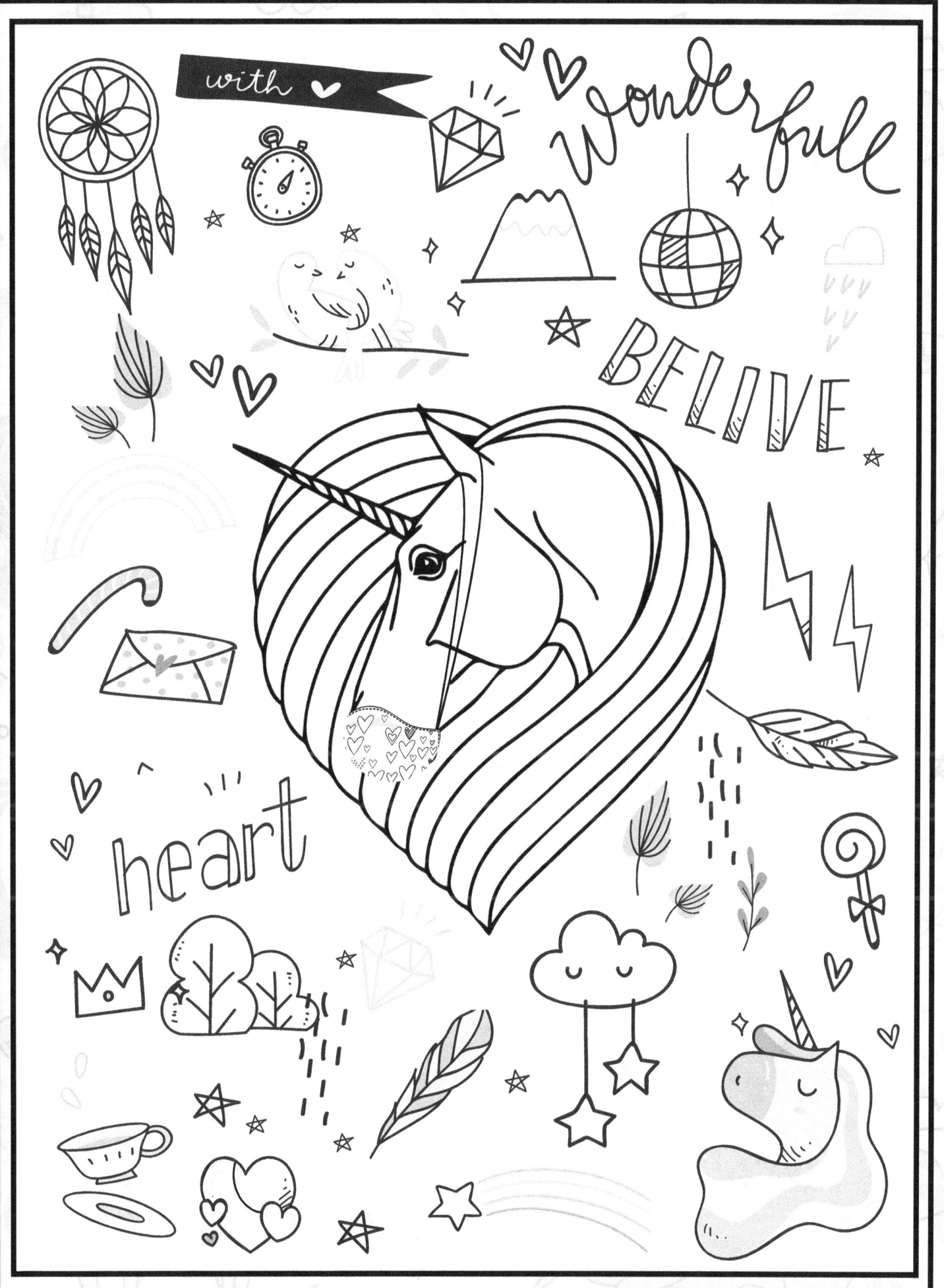

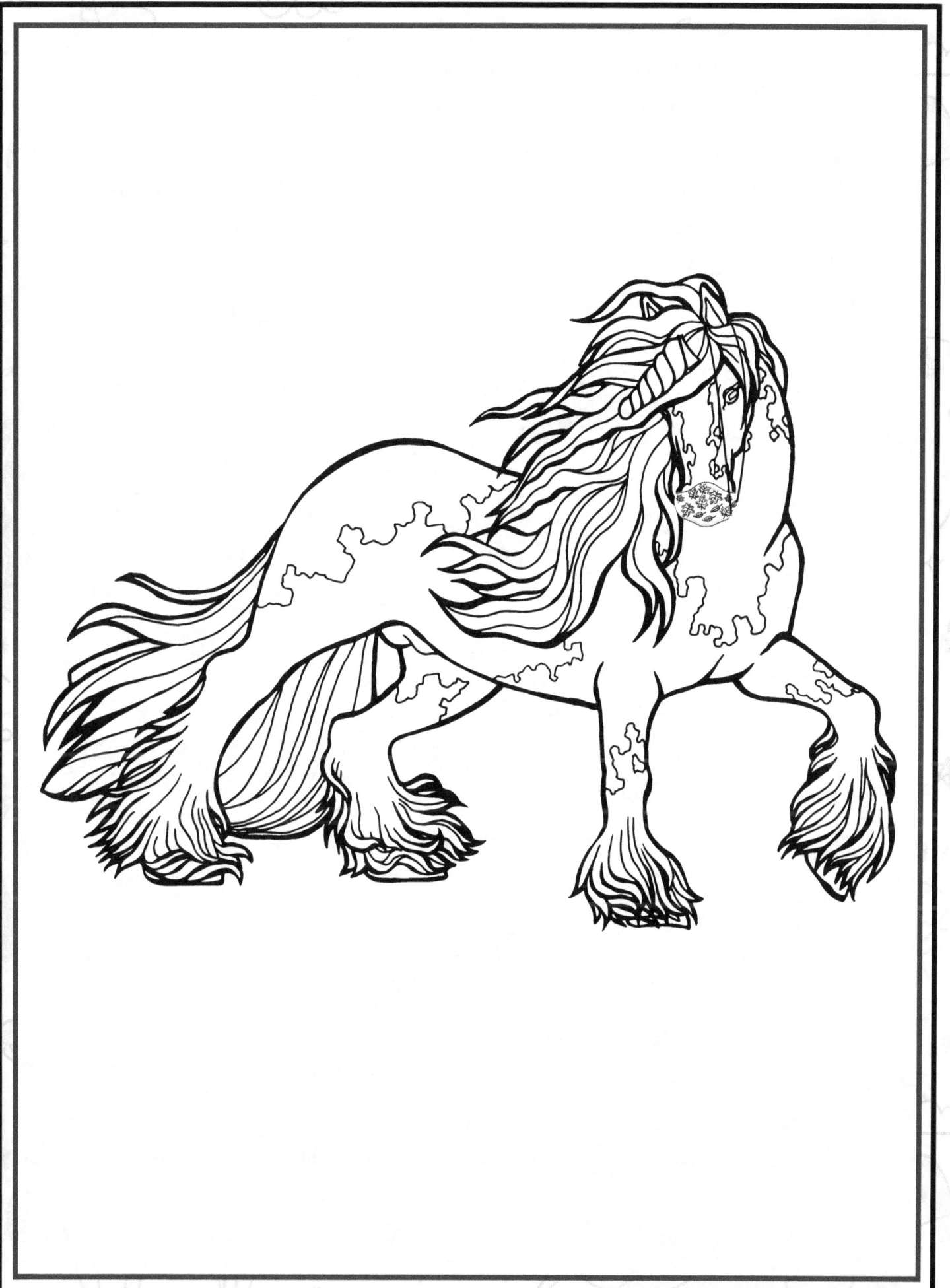

Maze 6

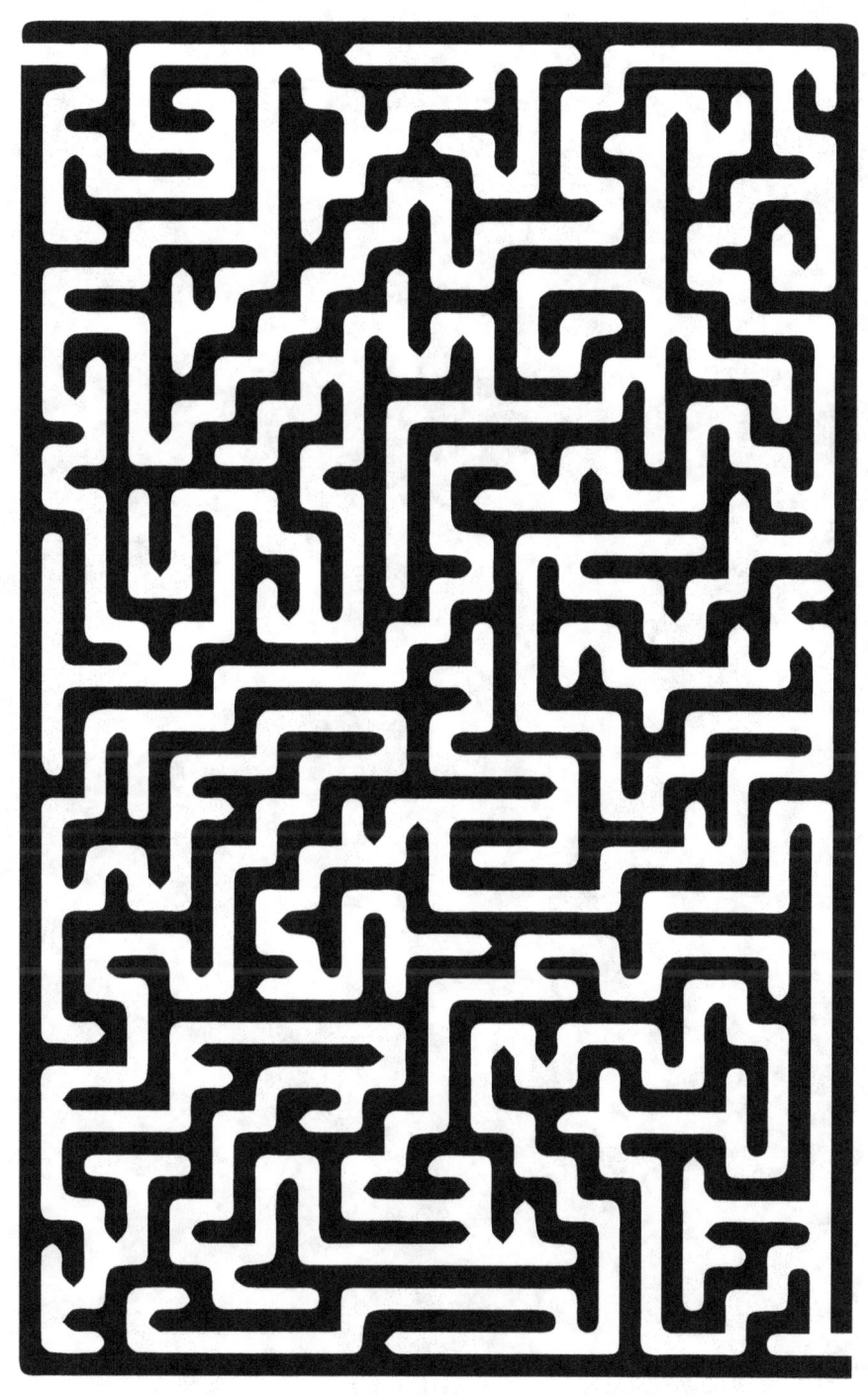

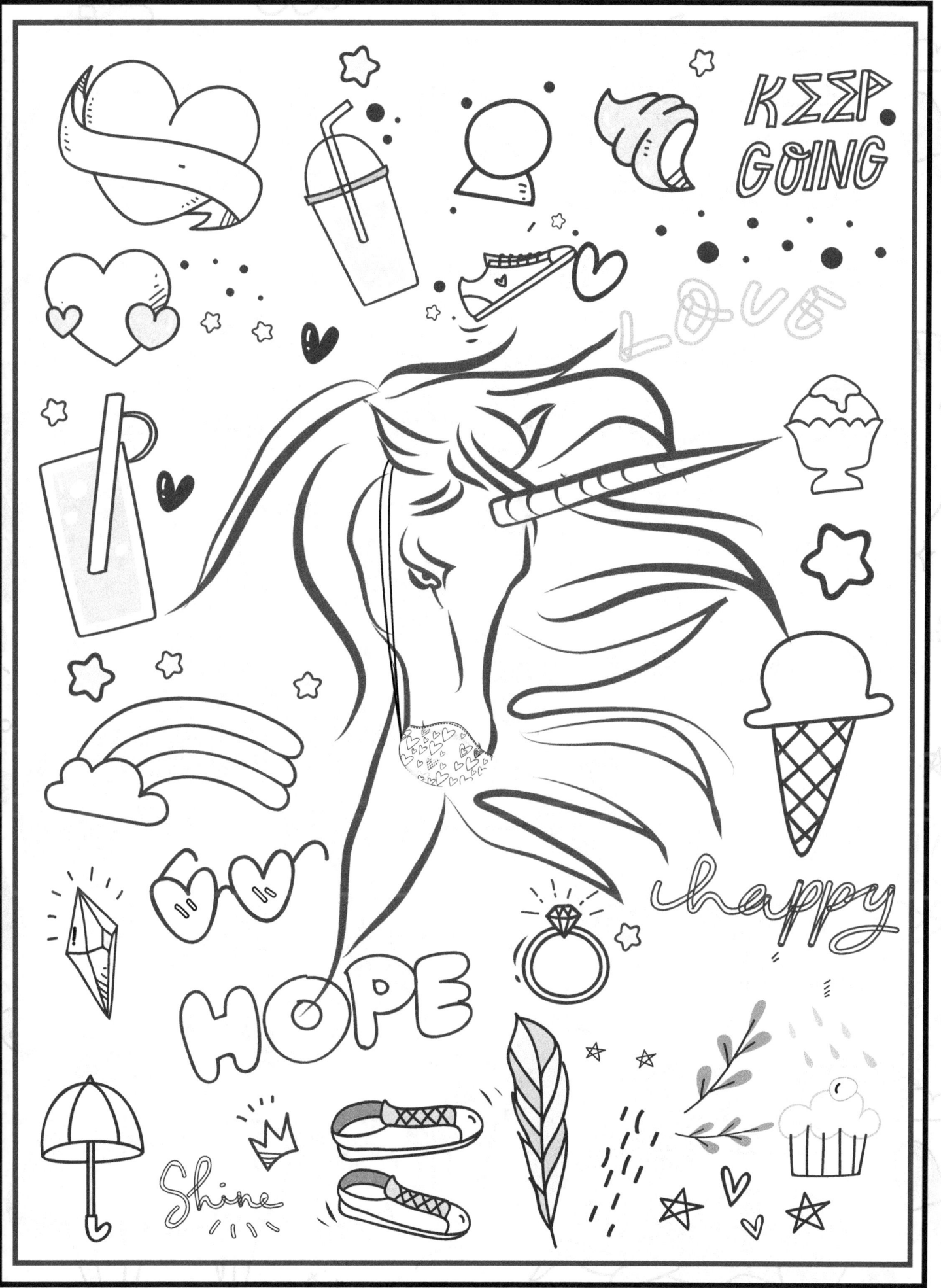

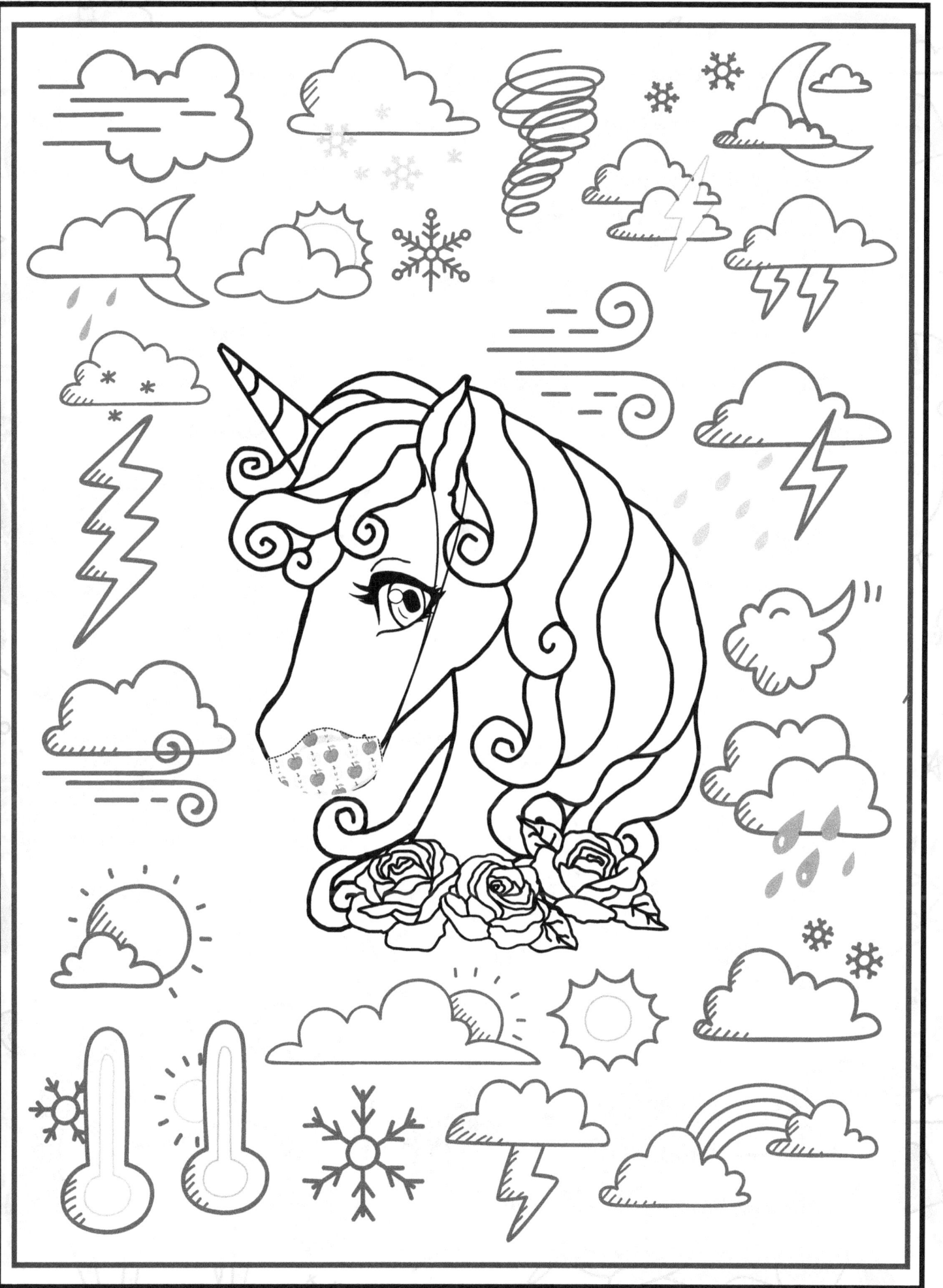

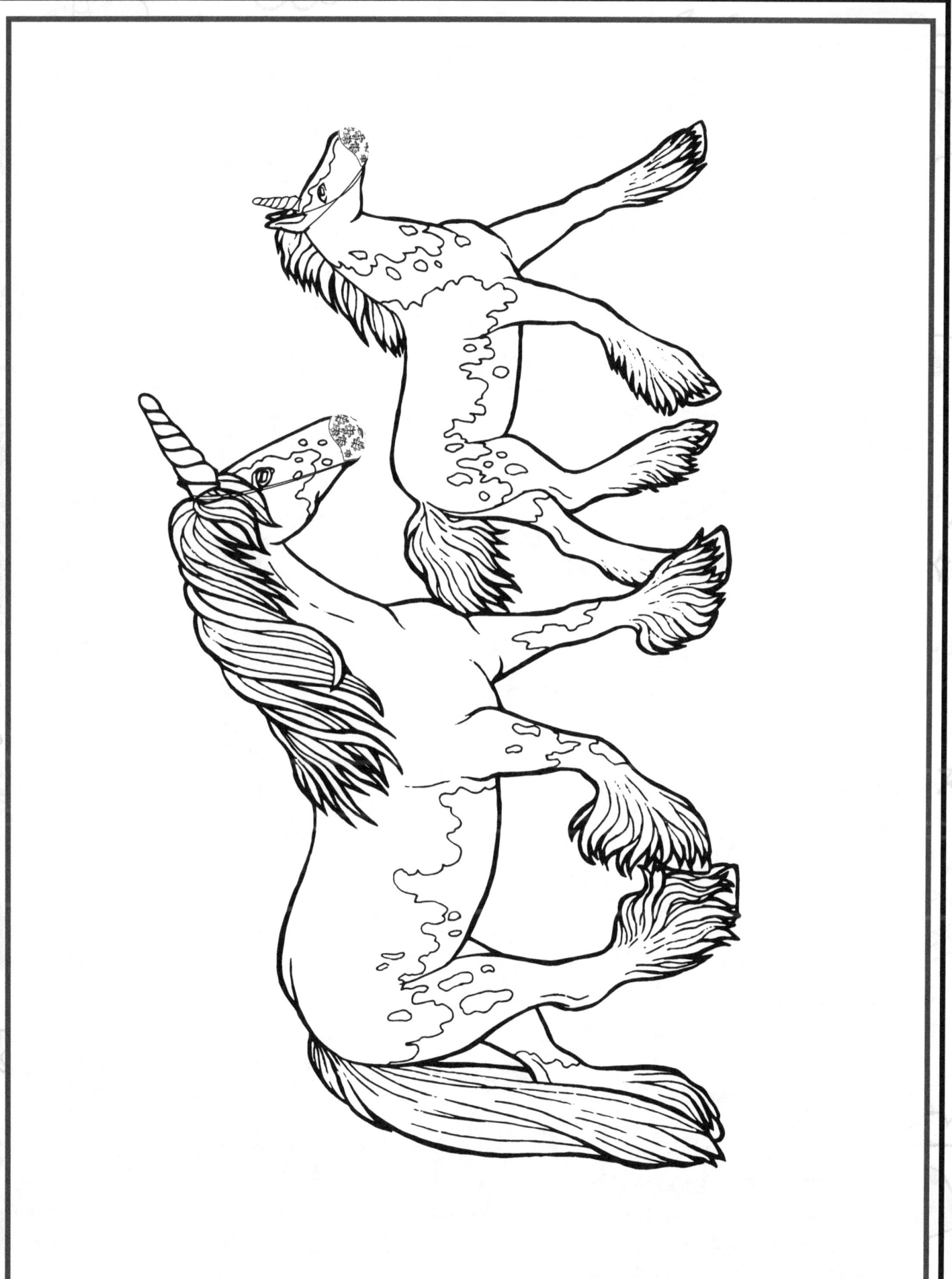

Maze 7

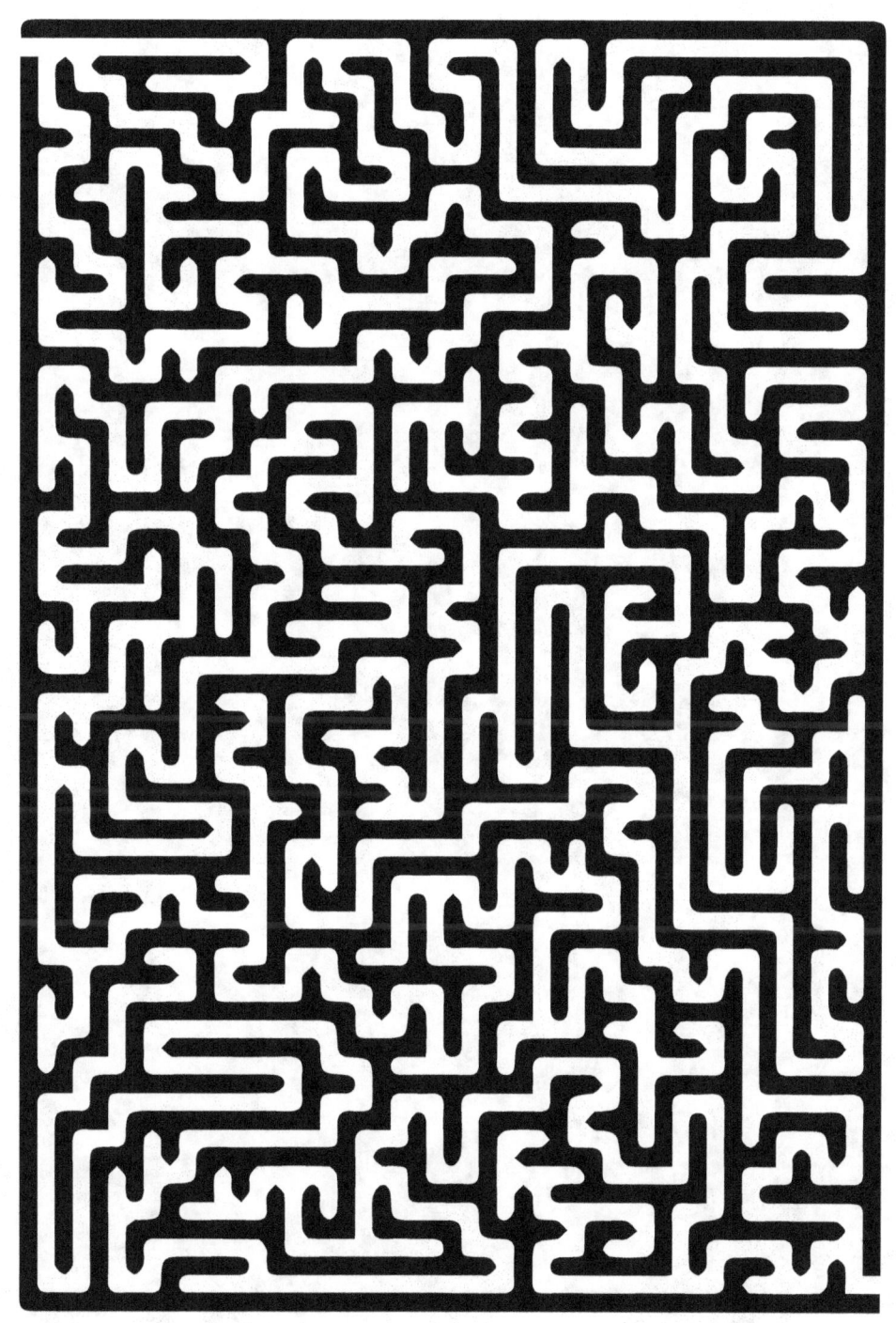

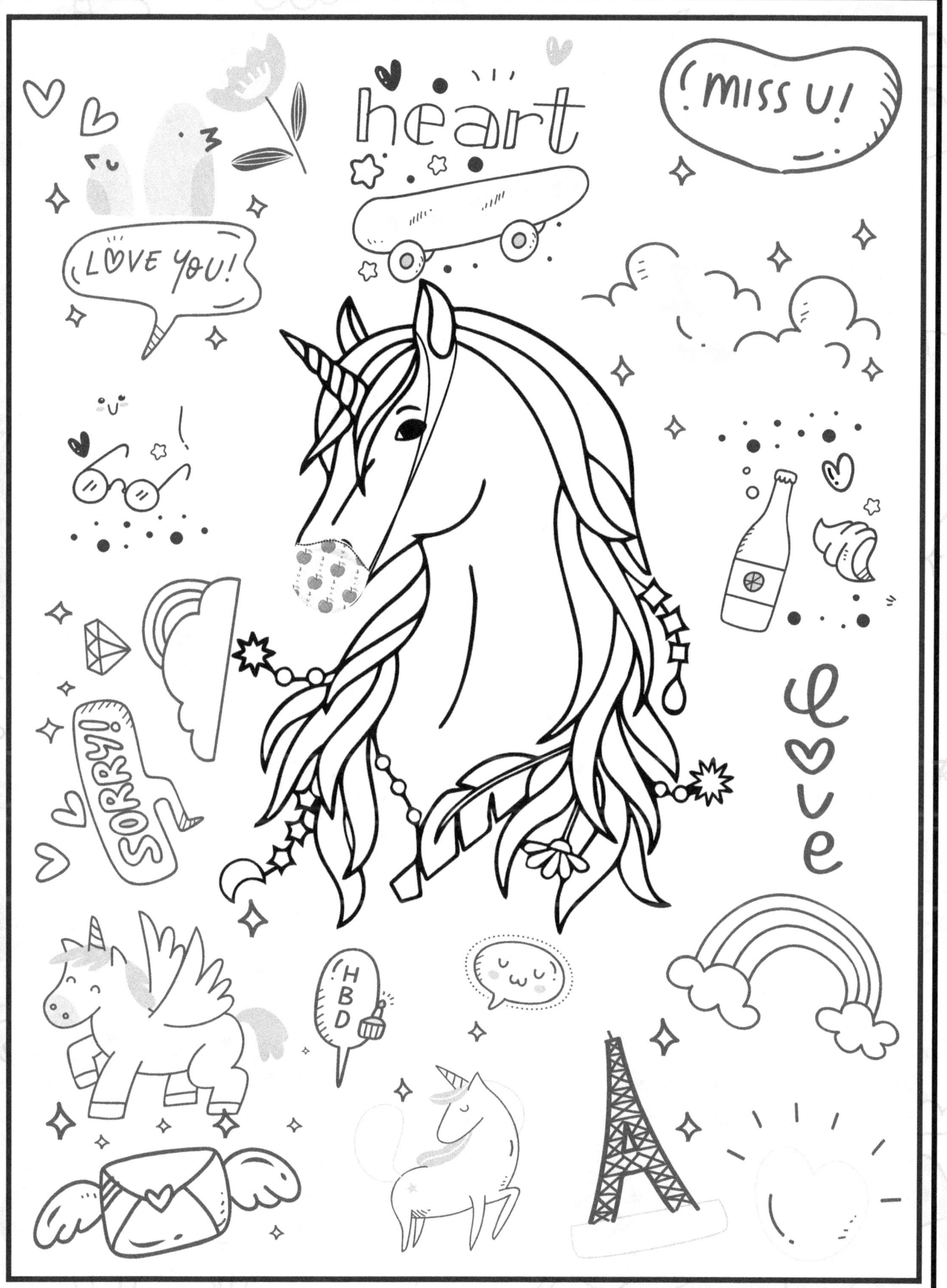

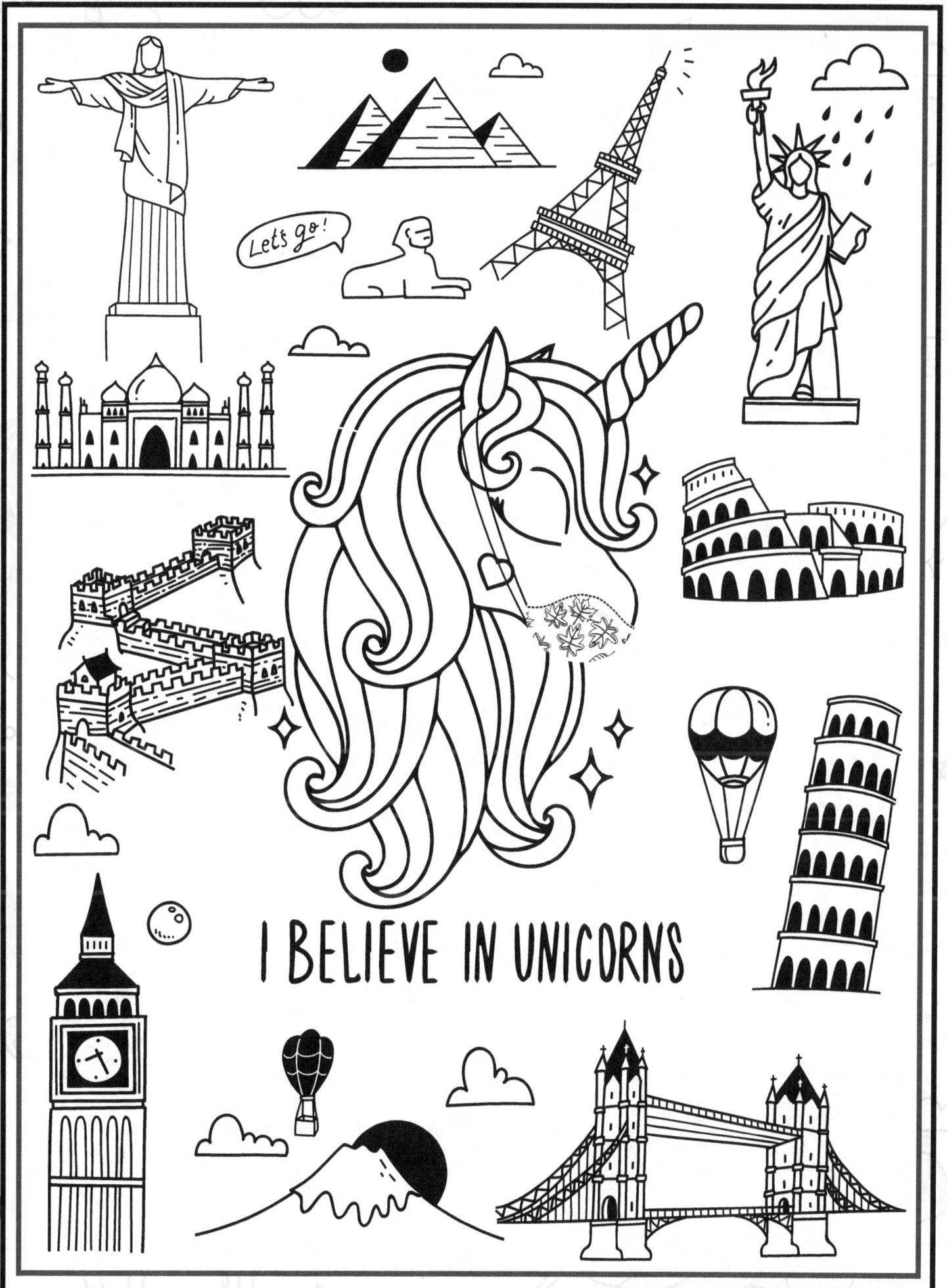

Maze 8

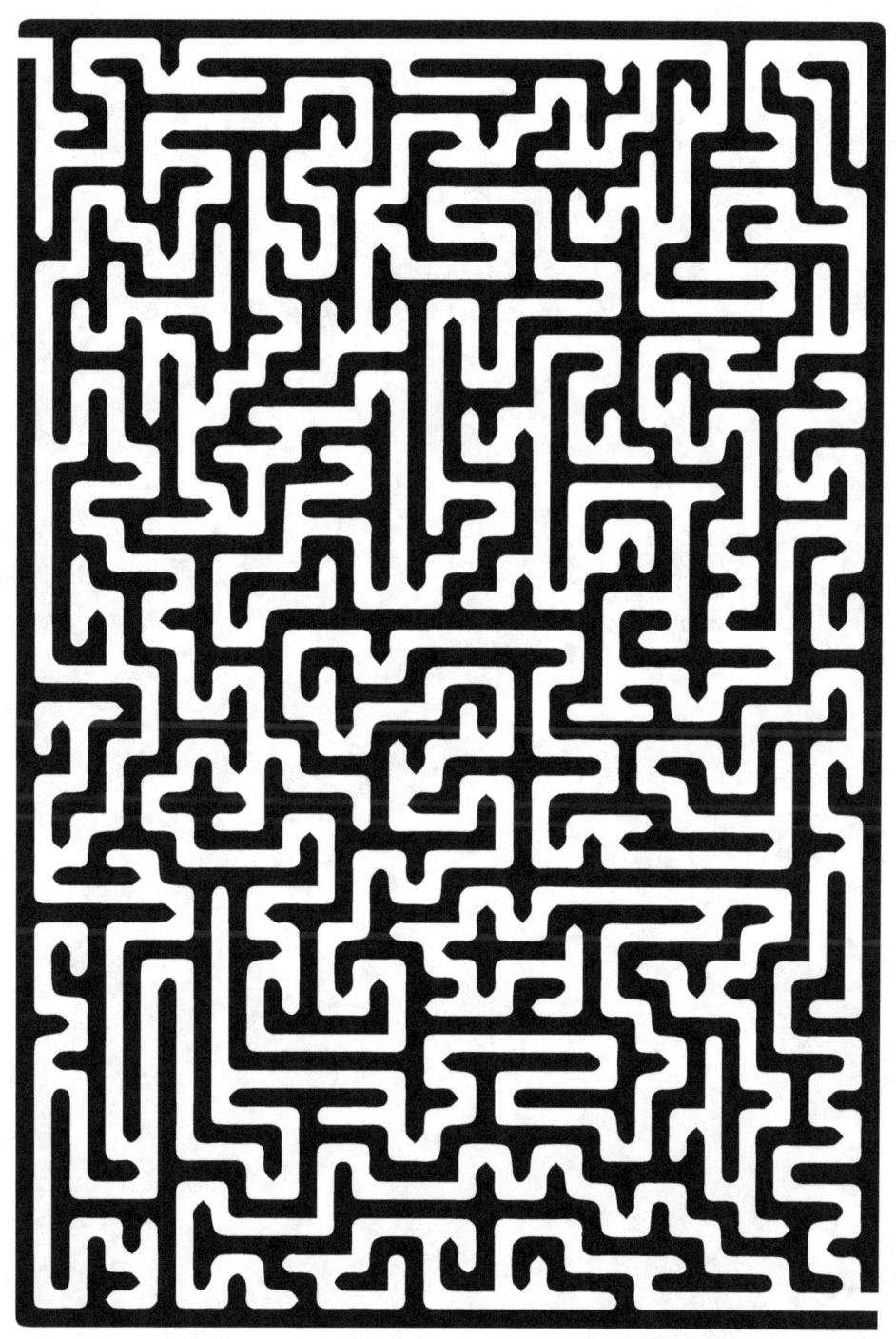

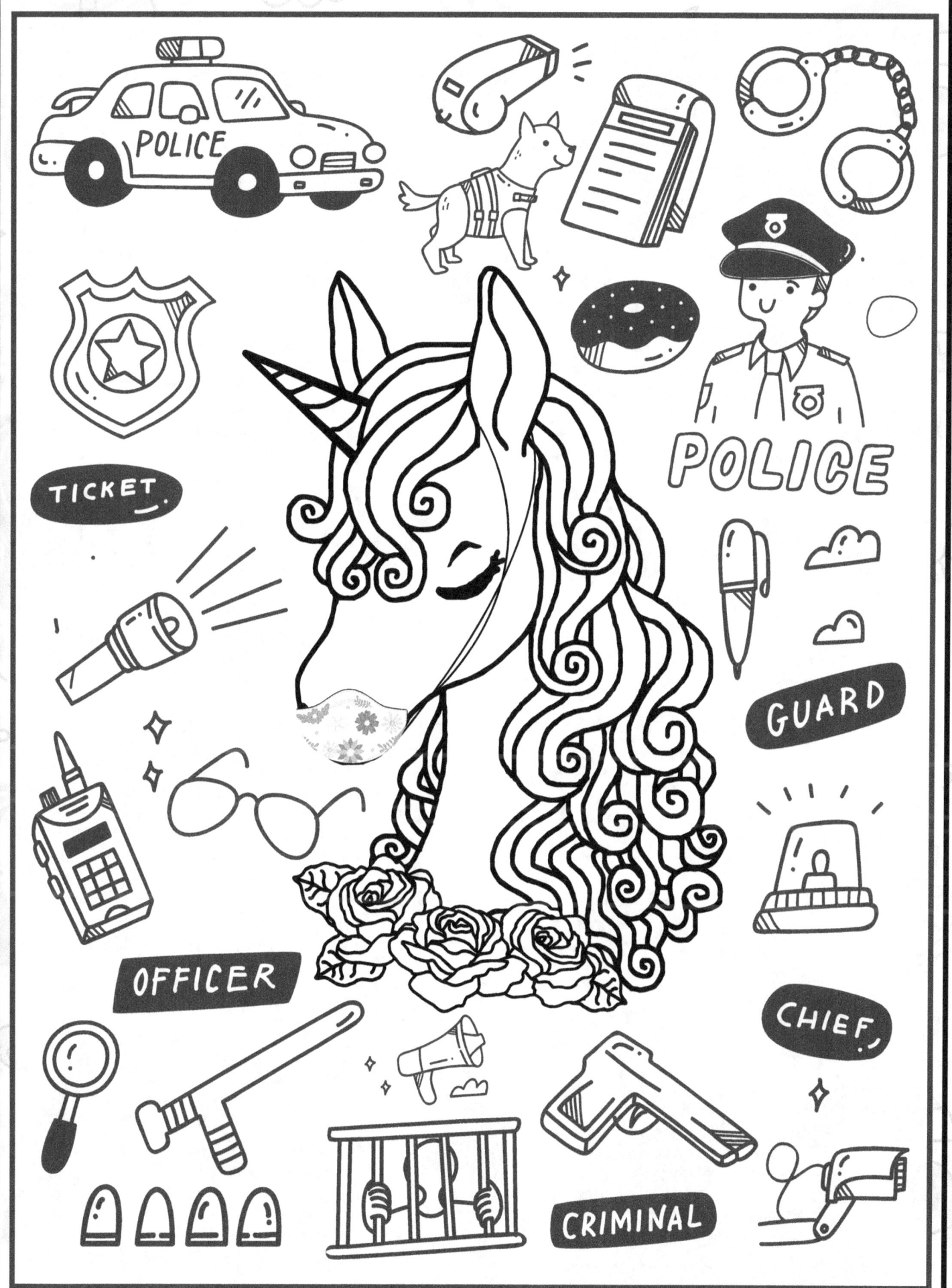

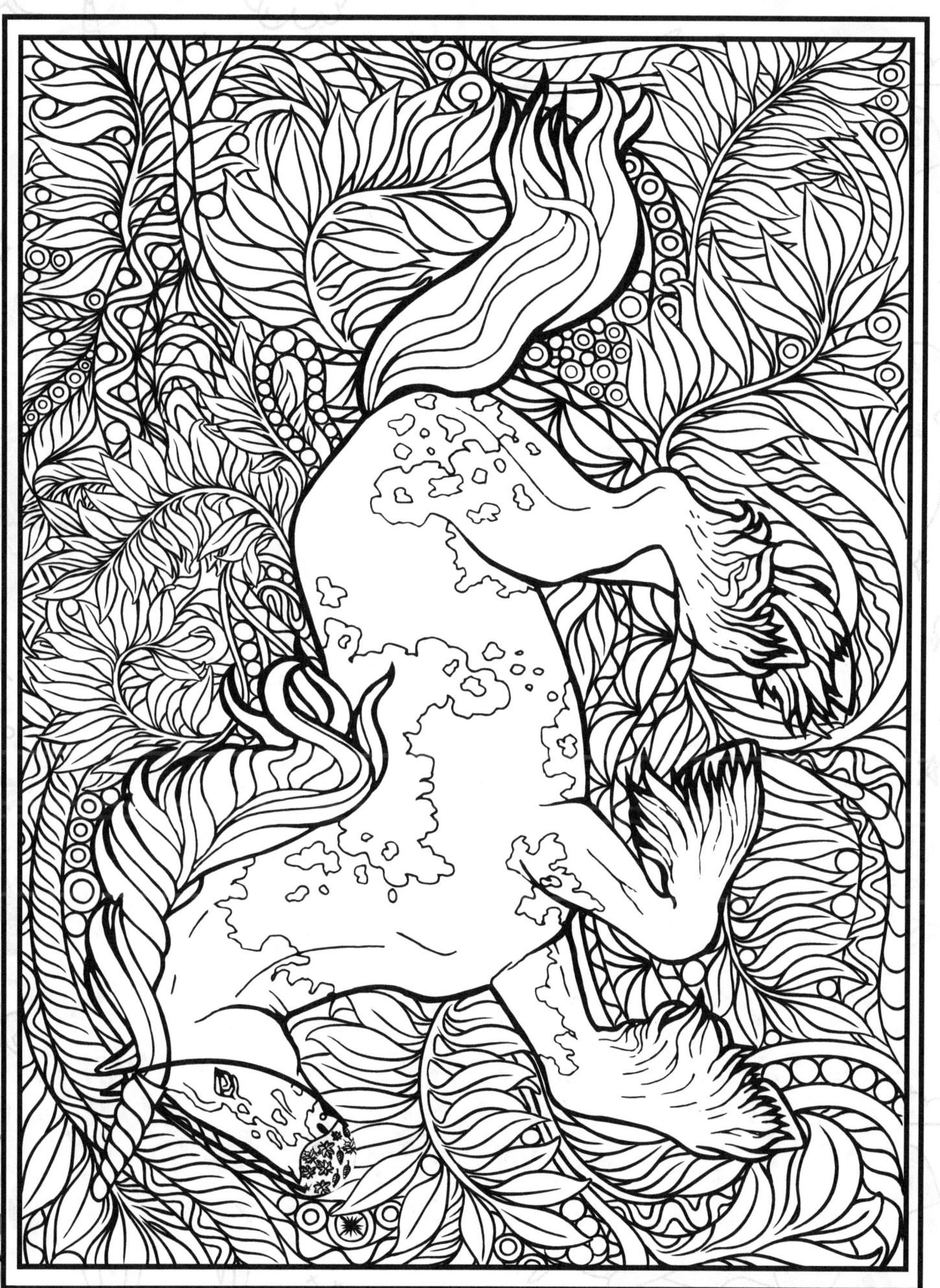

Congratulations you did it.

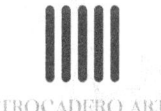
TROCADERO ART

Copyright © 2020 By H. Elmir

All rights reserved. This book or parts thereof may not be reproduced in any form, stored in any retrieval system, or transmitted in any form by any means electronic, mechanical, photocopy, recording, or otherwise without prior written permission of the publisher, except as provided by United States of America copyright law.

ISBN: 9798588002431

Printed by AMAZON.
www.amazon.com